MW00417196

"Daniel King is living the life he proclaims in *The Secret of Obed-Edom*. His clear writing will help you enjoy the presence of God and share His love everywhere you go. You were born for a purpose and designed to walk in God's blessing. The truth of God's Word relating the life of Obed-Edom is powerful. You can rise into a new dimension of victory and prosperity by applying what is written in this book."

—Pastor Billy Joe Daugherty, Victory Christian Center, Tulsa, OK

"*The Secret of Obed-Edom* is a powerful message that impacted people's lives in my church in the areas of servanthood, faithfulness, commitment, and not giving up...people were inspired to go after the things of God."

—Dr. Phillip Goudeaux, Calvary Christian Center, Sacramento, CA

"I was impressed how Obed-Edom's entire family was promoted along with him...wow! All his children and grandchildren served God because of his example."

—Sue Horst, mother of seven children

"This book should be read by everyone. It is required reading for anyone who is depressed, discouraged, or disillusioned with life."

—Dr. Larry Ollison, Walk on the Water Faith Church
Osage Beach, MO

"As a businessman who has helped run several multimillion dollar companies, I can verify that the principles found in this book will work!"

—Morgan Hill, President, First Seniors Financial Group, Atlanta, GA

"Daniel King did an outstanding job encouraging the people in our church to get involved with his message on Obed-Edom."

—Dr. Bracken Christian, Family Harvest Church, Lubbock, TX

"*The Secret of Obed-Edom* is a profound book. Every leader needs it. Every born-again believer needs it. Anybody who is trying to go further than where they are right now needs this book. You really need this book."

—**Bishop Larry Smith,** Abundant Faith World Ministries
Memphis, TN

"Daniel was a complete blessing to our church family. His teaching on Obed-Edom is the best I have ever heard. The response from our people was awesome."

—**Pastor Dominic Russo,** Oakland Christian Church
Oakland Township, MI

"Daniel, we've had so many comments from people in the congregation and how much they really appreciate you and your message on Obed-Edom. You impacted their lives!"

—**Pastor Kenneth Leleux,** Glorious Church Worship Center
New Iberia, LA

"I really believe that Daniel King's message on Obed-Edom will bring our whole church up another level."

—**Pastor Travis Burke,** New Life International Outreach Center
Tallahassee, FL

"Your revelatory message of the story of Obed-Edom and the way God will promote everyone despite their background, their past and/or occupation as long as their hearts are in tune with His, was awe-inspiring and touched our spirits immensely."

—Montego Bay, Jamaica

"I am greatly impressed with your team. It is certainly unique. God is using you to reach so many tens of thousands of people."

—**Dr. T. L. Osborn**—International Statesman and Evangelist

"Daniel King represents a new generation of missionary evangelists...he brings a tremendous spiritual heritage to his ministry, where integrity and faithfulness are the norm."

—**Pastor Billy and Marianne Allen**
Christ for the Nations Church—Dallas, TX

What are people saying about Daniel King's Other books?

Healing Power

"This is one of the best books I have ever read on healing."

—Mike Murdock

"I loved this book and I think you will, too."

—Marilyn Hickey

Fire Power

"Daniel King is a young man on fire for God."

—Billy Joe Daugherty

"In this book, Daniel shares how he keeps his 'red-hot' relationship with God."

—Charles Nieman

The Power of the Seed

"...I was impressed with the understanding Daniel has on this subject."

—Robb Thompson

"...Interesting read as well as being a great textbook on the Seed..."

—John Avanzini

Soulwinning

"I have seen Daniel King in action and the book exudes the same passion for people that you notice when you spend time with the author."

—Peter Youngren

THE SECRET OF OBED-EDOM

DANIEL KING

The Secret of Obed-Edom
ISBN: 1-931810-05-2
Copyright © 2008 by Daniel King
King Ministries International
P. O. Box 701113
Tulsa, OK 74170-1113 USA
1-877-431-4276
www.kingministries.com

Published by
Thorncrown Publishing
A Division of Yorkshire Publishing Group
7707 East 111th Street South, Suite 104
Tulsa, Oklahoma 74133
www.yorkshirepublishing.com

TABLE OF CONTENTS

INTRODUCTION:

YOUR STORY IS ABOUT TO BEGIN

"…God had blessed Obed-Edom…."

(1 CHRONICLES 26:5)

The first response when you hear this unusual name is, Who was Obed-Edom? The second and third questions you might ask are, Why was he blessed? What was the secret to his success? As a preacher my heart was stirred to ask, What lessons can be learned from his life? And will God bless you and me in the same way?

Growing up in church, I often heard messages about Abraham, Moses, and David, great godly heroes who changed history. Their stories inspired and encouraged me. Yet, even though the character of Obed-Edom was never the subject of one of my Sunday school lessons, in the last few years his example has shaped the way I live my life more than any other person!

Bruce Wilkerson wrote a best-selling book about another obscure Bible character, *The Prayer of Jabez*. While reading his book, I was struck by the tremendous life lessons Bruce was able to pull from only two verses of God's Scriptures. Amazed by the truth he discovered, I wondered if there were other people in the Bible I had never heard of who could also really impact my life.

I began by reading the long lists of names in the Bible, which were really boring. For several days I struggled through the dry task of reading long genealogies until I came across these words, "God had blessed Obed-Edom." I examined the names of the other people in the long register. Nothing was even hinted about them being blessed. As I continued to read, this one name stood out as a man God chose to bless, and it really got my attention. Why was this one particular man singled out as *the one* who was blessed? And, where had I heard that name before? I pulled out my laptop and typed his name into a Bible search program.

The name of Obed-Edom appears nineteen times in the *New International Version* of the Bible. I had to admit I was intrigued, and like a Bible sleuth I began to track down clues about this obscure Bible personality. As I searched his inspiring story, I found that I was learning some great life lessons. I couldn't stop reading and probing for every clue about this man's incredibly blessed life!

Not too long ago, I was invited to preach at a church in Dallas, Texas. When the pastor asked what text I would be sharing from, I enthusiastically began to tell him about my message, "The Secret of Obed-Edom." He quizzically asked, "Obed who?"

This is the response I repeatedly receive when I talk about Obed-Edom and you've probably never heard of him either. That's okay. I've talked to long-time Bible scholars who were unable to remember who he was. But his story is so powerful and wonderful that I know it will be a tremendous blessing to your life.

I preached this message at one particular church on Wednesday night, and immediately the pastor asked me to return to preach the exact same message the following Sunday morning. Not only that, the pastor of the largest church in Central America also heard me preach on Obed-Edom and invited me to preach that night to his congregation of thirty thousand people. The truth is, everywhere I have preached this sermon, I have heard remarkable reports about how the story of Obed-Edom has changed people's lives.

When I started my research into Obed-Edom's life, I never dreamed that a crowd of thirty thousand people would one day be listening to me tell the remarkable and compelling story of his life. This story has impacted so many lives, I felt impressed by the Holy Spirit to write the account in this book, so that you, too, can activate the secret of Obed-Edom in your own life.

While I cannot physically share this message with everyone in the world, a book has the power to go to the nations. It can have a great influence in many arenas of life; the desk of a professor, the lap of a refugee, or the coffee table of a President! Only God Himself knows where this book will end up! Because you now hold this story in your own hands, I believe God wants to bless you in the same way he blessed Obed-Edom.

Although the principles in Obed-Edom's story are ancient, they have been repeated a million times down through the centuries. In fact, in my experience, I have never met a successful person who has not taken a similar path to Obed-Edom's. As you follow the simple principles outlined in this book, you too can experience the same rewards. Obed-Edom's story is universal and as we explore his life together in the following pages, you too will discover the same time-honored secrets to living the life of your dreams.

Perhaps you don't believe that you are a candidate for blessings of this magnitude. Well, I believe this book has found its way into your life for that exact purpose, so that you can be blessed in the same way Obed-Edom was blessed. Obed-Edom was not widely known, yet God still blessed him and changed his life for the better. God is no respecter of persons and He will do the same for you.

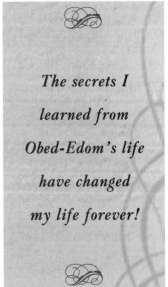

The secrets I learned from Obed-Edom's life have changed my life forever!

The secrets I learned from Obed-Edom's life have changed my life forever! I will never be the same, and neither will you as you experience the transformational truths in this book for yourself.

Are you ready for the secret of Obed-Edom to be activated in your life?

Well, here's how his marvelous story begins...

CHAPTER 1

WHEN GOD MOVES IN

*"[King David] did not take the ark to be with him
in the city of David. Instead, he took it aside
to the house of Obed-Edom...."*

(1 CHRONICLES 13:13)

"Daddy, a parade is coming!" squealed Shemaiah. Obed-Edom looked up from the broken plow as his firstborn son bounded excitedly into the barn. Engrossed in the busyness of planting crops, taking care of the herd, and trying to feed his family, he distractedly responded, "Shem, there is little time to go and watch a parade."

"Please, Father," Shemaiah begged, "can't you hear the music and see the camels? Can we just take a quick look? It's so exciting!"

Obed-Edom sighed begrudgingly to himself thinking, *Another caravan has caught Shemaiah's attention!* "Son, can't you see that I'm busy?" he responded in a last-ditch effort to convince his precocious child that he didn't have time to play.

"But, Daddy, look at all the dancing and singing! They're playing harps and tambourines; cymbals are clanging and trumpets are blaring! I've never seen so many people in one place. It's the biggest parade in the whole wide world and it's coming right down our road! Please, Daddy?"

Just as Shemaiah finished speaking, Obed-Edom heard the tumultuous roar of distant shouting, "Long live King David! Long live the king!" The sound of the thundering chorus was so intense it startled them both and aroused Obed-Edom's curiosity.

Grabbing his son by the hand, the pair bolted outdoors, their eyes squinting in response to the bright sunlight. "Well," Obed-Edom said as they made their way toward a better view of the commotion, "if the king is coming, we might as well see him for ourselves. Come, son, let's meet this royal procession!"

The path to Obed-Edom's house was right beside the busy road that led into Jerusalem, the new capital of the kingdom of Israel. King David had made this mountaintop city his residence, and this dusty road now hustled and bustled with government officials dispatching the king's business.

As Obed-Edom gazed down the valley at the curving mountain road, he watched as a massive crowd of people emerged from a cloud of dust, rays of sunshine outlining their dancing forms. All restraint had been abandoned in their revelry. Shemaiah giggled as he pointed at their unbridled antics. The cheering throng continued past the threshing floor of Chidon and made their way up the dusty road to where he and his father stood.

As they continued to watch the spectacle, Obed-Edom noticed a large cart in front of the procession, pulled by a pair of oxen. The revelers' attention seemed focused on a beautiful golden box sitting high in the cart, brilliantly reflecting the light of the sun. Its gleam gave off an unearthly radiance as the oxen slowly plodded up the bumpy road.

"Excuse me," Obed-Edom interrupted, grabbing the sweaty, waving arm of a man caught up in the commotion and excitement, "what on earth is going on?"

"Huh?" the man loudly grunted over the noise of the clashing cymbals and beating drums.

Obed-Edom raised his voice over the uproar and yelled, "Why is everyone celebrating? What is going on?"

"Haven't you heard?" the astonished man replied. "King David is bringing the Ark of the Covenant back to Jerusalem where it belongs! The ark is coming home!"

Startled, Obed-Edom took a second look at the golden box precariously balanced on the cart and noticed the oxen were having difficulty maneuvering the worn-out road. He recognized the shapes of the two angelic figurines on its cover and remembered a conversation he had with his father years earlier. "Son, let me tell you about Israel's holiest artifact, the Ark of the Covenant. It is fashioned of quality acacia wood and overlaid in pure gold! One of the finest craftsmen in the kingdom, Bezalel, was chosen to make it according to precise instructions given by God to Moses. Think about it, son, the exact details were given by Jehovah Himself, so that God could live among us. God's literal presence dwells inside the Ark of the Covenant."

As the pageant of thousands passed Obed-Edom's house, he was astonished to see King David himself leading the dancers! Just like his followers, he too spun and leaped with complete abandonment, reveling in the joyous music and the merry hearts of his people. The fervor and excitement stirred Obed-Edom to the core with an inexplicable yearning to join in the celebration himself.

Suddenly, the ark shifted from its position on the back of the cart as one of the oxen stumbled on the rocky road. One wheel creaked under the strain of the uneven weight, while the other wheel slipped into a pothole the frantic driver valiantly attempted to avoid. Obed-Edom gasped as he helplessly watched the sacred golden box slide out of the back of the cart toward the ground. The Ark of the Covenant was heading for disaster!

An alert young man dancing near the ark reacted immediately to the pending calamity. He instinctively reached out his hand to prevent the ark from falling and was able to halt its sudden descent. But just as suddenly, he collapsed to the ground stricken by some invisible force, and lay unmoving in the dust. The crowd gasped as the music quickly ground to a halt; horrified spectators gathered around his still form. Rushing to him, a hysterical young woman bent down and turned his lifeless body over. She screamed, "He's dead! Uzzah's dead! I can't believe it! It can't be true!"

"What happened, Daddy?" Shemaiah asked tearfully, looking up at Obed-Edom with round eyes like orbs.

"I don't know, Shem. Stay here while I find out."

Obed-Edom mingled among the stunned crowd, quietly asking anyone for enlightenment. "What just happened here? I don't understand; why did Uzzah die?"

"He touched the ark!" an awestruck man responded. "No one is supposed to touch the Ark of the Covenant. He was foolish enough to touch it without thinking of the consequences!"

The terrified crowd parted silently as King David made his way toward the dead young man's body. As he fell to his knees, he cried out in anguish, "Lord, forgive me! Oh God, please forgive me."

With tears streaming from his eyes, the king stood with a heavy heart and announced, "The celebration is over. Everyone go home. Go back to your villages and families."

"But what should we do with the ark, your majesty?" a timid musician asked the king.

"Just leave it here," David replied flatly.

"Here, in the middle of the road?"

"No, not here," the king replied shaking his head in grieving disbelief. "Put it in that house over there."

Obed-Edom's jaw dropped. The king was pointing at his house. *Can I truly believe what I'm hearing? My humble house for the Ark of the Covenant?* thought Obed-Edom. *My dwelling for the ark covered in pure gold! My house for the holiest artifact in the nation of Israel?*

He approached the king with hesitation. "Please, your majesty, my dwelling is not worthy to keep the Ark of the Covenant."

King David's eyes flashed with annoyed anger. He repeated the command, "Take the ark into this man's home and leave it there for now."

As the crowd dispersed, the ark was lifted by its wooden poles and carried gingerly up the path to Obed-Edom's home.

The enormity of what had happened flashed through Obed-Edom's mind. *What will it be like to have God's presence in my house?* pondered Obed-Edom as he followed the ark through his front gate. *What will happen when Almighty God, the Creator of the heavens and the earth, comes to dwell in my humble dwelling? What will it be like to have the glory of God in the midst of my home?* He shook with wonder and trepidation as he grasped Shemaiah's smaller hand.

When God Moves
Into "Your House!"

Imagine God the all-powerful, all-knowing, all-loving Creator of the universe moving into your spare bedroom!

"Mr. God," you say hesitantly while giving Him a tour of your home, "please help Yourself to anything in the fridge. I put towels out for You on the bed. *Mi casa es su casa.* My house is Your house. Please make Yourself at home. If there is anything, anything at all that I can do for You, please don't hesitate to let me know."

God chuckles, "No, My child, if there is anything I can do for you, just ask! By the way, you don't need to call Me "Mister." Just call Me 'Father;' I'm here to help you."

God wants to use all of heaven's assets, the fullness of His infinite wisdom and the abundance of His miracle power to make your life the absolute best it can possibly be. The adventure begins when you invite God to come and dwell in your house. The greatest miracle you can ever experience is the miracle of God's presence living within you.

Here are some questions to reflect on:

1. Are you dissatisfied with your life?
2. Are you bored with the normal humdrum of everyday living?
3. Do you long for something more?
4. Do you face insurmountable problems?
5. Do you ever feel depressed?
6. Do you long to accomplish something significant?

If you will invite God to live within you, He will help you answer all the questions you have felt but have never been able to articulate. If you have ever desired something more out of life and haven't known where to look, this book of Obed-Edom's unique story will help point you in the right direction.

God has a great plan for your life. He does not want you to be satisfied with where you are. God wants to take you to a new level of living. You can have more out of life. You can have more joy, more meaning, more satisfaction, more peace, and more prosperity. You can experience a better marriage, find a better job, and enjoy greater contentment than ever before.

From Visitation to Habitation

We should move from inviting God to "visit" our house to asking God to "live" in our house. Typically, we invite God to visit at bedtime, mealtimes, or perhaps in a time of crisis, but God wants to live with us all the time.

Experiencing a life of blessing begins when God comes to live in your house. Obed-Edom's life was radically changed when God's presence entered his home.

How do I know God's presence will change your life for the better? His track record is phenomenal! The Bible is full of people whose lives were radically improved because of God's presence.

- Abraham and Sarah were given a son
- Joseph was promoted to a position of leadership in Egypt
- Moses led the Israelites to the promised land
- Joshua won the battle of Jericho

- ✎ Hannah conceived

- ✎ Elijah saw fire fall from heaven

- ✎ David became king

- ✎ Solomon was granted wisdom and became wealthy

- ✎ Daniel was delivered from a den of hungry lions

- ✎ Mary became the mother of Jesus

All of these great men and women of God have one common denominator. Each one invited God to be a significant part of their lives.

God Wants to Live with You

Of all the miracles in the Bible, none are as exciting to me as the blessing Obed-Edom experienced when God came to live in his house. Why? The answer is simple. Because inviting the presence of God into your life is the greatest moment in your life. God isn't just visiting you; He inhabits you. You become His dwelling place.

In the time of Obed-Edom, God's presence literally inhabited the golden box known as the Ark of the Covenant. This box was kept hidden from the people and no one had access to the presence of God. However, God never intended for His presence to be hidden from His people.

In the beginning of time, God created the first man and woman, Adam and Eve, to be His friends. Every day in the Garden of Eden, God walked and talked with them. But one day they disobeyed God. This sin of disobedience caused them to lose fellowship with God. No longer were they able to walk and talk with Him. Suddenly they were cut off from God's presence.

The Ark of the Covenant was built as a visible reminder of the relationship Adam and Eve once had with God. As the priests of Israel carried the ark, it reminded the people that God wants to walk and talk with humankind. This desire was fulfilled when Jesus Christ, the Son of God, was born in the city of Bethlehem two thousand years ago. Through Jesus, God once again walked among us and talked with us. When Jesus died on a cross, He paid the price for the sins of humankind and made it possible for us once again to enter into the presence of God.

Just like Obed-Edom's life was radically changed when God's presence entered his home, your life will drastically improve when you invite Jesus to come and live with you. Remember, Scripture explains to us that our body is the temple (house) of God.

In Old Testament times, the presence of God was confined to the ark, but because Jesus came, God's presence is now available to all of His creation. Today the ark is obsolete, but God's presence still moves into people's houses. We can all live as Obed-Edom's family did, with a tangible sense of God's presence in our homes.

God is more than a religious belief, or an icon on the wall, or a deity to mumble prayers to before eating a meal, or a list of rules to live by, or someone whose meetings we attend. He is our friend. God wants to walk with you and talk with you on a daily basis. His greatest desire is to have a relationship with you. God created you to be His friend. When you invite God's presence into your house, you can experience the same miracles Obed-Edom experienced!

God created you to be His friend.

The Hebrew word for "presence" means "face," "in front of," or "to see one's face." When my wife wants my attention, she sits on my lap and with a hand on my cheek turns my face to look her in the eyes. She enjoys my presence as much as I enjoy hers. Being in God's presence simply means spending time with Him, talking to Him "face-to-face."

The greatest gift God has given you is His presence. The greatest gift we can give God is a desire to be in His presence. We reveal our desire for God's presence by the amount of time we spend seeking Him. Pursuit is proof of desire!

Seek God's face, not His hand.

Many make the mistake of only seeking God's blessing instead of celebrating His presence. It is important to seek God's face, not His hand. We love God because of Who He is, not because of what He has done or can do for us. God is not an eternal Santa Claus. We should chase His presence, not His presents. It should not be just "I want blessings from God." It should be, "I want God." The marvelous thing about seeking the Giver is that when you find Him, you also receive His gifts simply because He loves you.

What Can God's Presence Do for You?

My calling as a preacher and author is to introduce people to God. In over fifty nations around the world, I have helped usher individuals into the presence of God. In every country, in every culture, in every age group, across the full spectrum of economic status and educational levels, from presidents of nations to peasants in mud huts, I have seen God's presence make a difference in many people's lives and I know it will in yours!

In God's presence...

Your past is erased.

Your future is revealed.

Your enemies are exposed.

Your lack has to get back.

Your pain can't remain.

Your fear must disappear.

Your sins are washed away.

Your weakness turns to strength.

Your priorities are put in proper order.

Your poverty becomes abundance.

Your depression turns to joy.

Your flawed thinking is corrected.

Your identity as a child of God is revealed.

Your destiny is discovered.

In God's presence you will find:

- Abundance (John 10:10)
- Comfort (Isaiah 51:12)
- Deliverance (Psalm 34:19)
- Encouragement (2 Thessalonians 2:16)
- Favor (Proverbs 12:2)
- Forgiveness (Psalm 103:3)
- Healing (Exodus 15:26)
- Joy (Psalm 16:11)
- Love (1 John 4:8)
- Patience (Psalm 37:7)

- Peace (John 14:27)

- Protection (Psalm 91)

- Prosperity (Psalm 25:12-13)

- Rest (Exodus 33:14)

- Strength (Nehemiah 8:10)

- Wisdom (Proverbs 2:6)

Do you want to discover the blessing of Obed-Edom by experiencing the miracle of God's presence? Right now, invite God to live in your house by praying this simple prayer: "Dear God, I invite You to come live in my house. I want to experience Your presence every day. Come walk with me and talk with me. I want You to be my friend. Amen."

So, God came to live in Obed-Edom's house, but guess what? His story and yours are not finished yet.

CHAPTER 2

THE BLESSING OF GOD

*"The ark of God remained with the family of
Obed-Edom in his house for three months, and
the Lord blessed his household and everything he had."*

(1 CHRONICLES 13:14)

How will God's presence change my family today? Obed-Edom sleepily wondered as he sat up in bed and yawned. He glanced down the hallway to the living room where the Ark of the Covenant was sitting larger than life. Some mornings he awoke grumpy and took it out on his wife when breakfast was not ready the moment he stomped into the kitchen and sat down. But today, he did not feel right about yelling at his wife in front of the ark. He knew God wanted him to love and care for his wife and family. He decided to be kind today. After all, the last person who disobeyed God's law by touching the ark had dropped dead!

Stepping inside the kitchen, Obed-Edom paused for a moment, enjoying the childish chatter of small voices and the comforting smell of gruel on the fire. For the first time he noticed how harried his wife seemed, feeding the squirming children and rushing to prepare his favorite breakfast.

"Wife," he boomed, clearing his throat, "I'm going to help feed the children while you're busy with my breakfast."

His wife turned in surprise with an eyebrow upraised. "Really?" she asked, incredulously, "I mean, thank you! I would really appreciate the help." Obed-Edom grinned as he spooned gruel into his newborn's upturned mouth. He suspected she would find a way to reward him that night.

Obed-Edom's wife picked up a rag and began her household chores after he left to work in the field. After all, if God Himself was going to live in her home, it should be clean and spotless. She dusted the living room with caution, careful not to touch the ark. Her husband had explained in great detail how she was to make sure no one touched the golden box.

As Obed-Edom strolled through his fields perusing the crops, he was intrigued to find that tiny shoots had appeared overnight in his wheat fields. Not only had they appeared early, they were thicker than last year. As he contemplated possible reasons for the sudden growth, a familiar and unwelcome figure appeared. "Obed-Edom, do you remember selling me part of your herd last year?"

"Of course I remember," replied Obed-Edom indignantly, "you cheated me of half their value."

"I know," his neighbor confessed sheepishly, "I feel bad about what I did. I'm truly sorry. Here is full payment to make up for what I stole from you."

Obed-Edom was amazed! He hefted the cloth sack of money in his hand. *What would he do with this special windfall? I'm going to open a fruit stand beside the road to Jerusalem,* he decided. *The travelers passing by will be hungry, so I'll make a tent for them to rest in the shade awhile and refresh themselves.*

In the afternoon he labored with a cow, helping her deliver a mewling calf. The cow had miscarried several times before, but this newborn was healthy. He arranged immediately to sell the mother and her calf to another neighbor who needed a milk cow. He used the payment to purchase a nearby field he had his eye on. No sooner had he finished the transaction, a man appeared and announced, "I've wanted to buy that field for a long time. I'll give you double what you just paid for it!" Obed-Edom was both surprised and stunned. What on earth was going on? He had never been so blessed. *Why now?* he wondered.

That night Obed-Edom strolled into his home extremely happy with the day's profit. "Honey, how clean the house looks!" he said happily as first he embraced his wife and then handed her a lovely bunch of wildflowers.

"Guess what?" she said, "your firstborn passed his exam at school today with flying colors."

"Son, I'm proud of you," Obed-Edom said as he tossled Shemaiah's curly hair. "I've been thinking about this remarkable day and have concluded that the ark of God is bringing this incredible blessing to us. I must admit that yesterday when all the singing and dancing were going on I thought people were crazy acting like that because of an ark on a cart! And when I watched that young man die for only touching it I was puzzled and afraid. Even King David's command to bring it to our house made me apprehensive. But, now I finally understand that God blesses us when we obey the commands of both the king and our God. Let's take a moment to kneel in front of the ark and pray to Jehovah. We really have so much to be thankful for today." Shemaiah was the first to jump up and kneel before the Ark of the Covenant. Obed-Edom and his wife smiled at each other in silent satisfaction as they knelt down beside him with the rest of their children. Today, their entire family served God together!

Obed-Edom smiled as he drifted off contentedly to sleep, clasping hands with his wife under the covers. If today was any indicator of the blessings that came with God's presence, God was welcome to stay in his house forever!

How Can You Be Blessed?

Obed-Edom was blessed:

His family was blessed.

His marriage was blessed.

His business was blessed.

His real estate was blessed.

His kids were blessed.

His animals were blessed.

His crops were blessed.

His relationships were blessed.

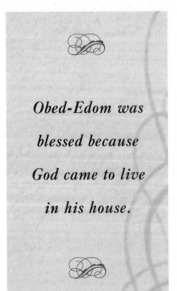

Obed-Edom was blessed because God came to live in his house.

Everything Obed-Edom owned and everything he touched was blessed. Why? For one simple reason. Obed-Edom was blessed because God came to live in his house.

Can you imagine having Dr. Phil as your marriage coach, Donald Trump as your real estate advisor, Billy Banks as your fitness instructor, Martha Stewart your home decorator, Bill Gates as your computer guru, and Warren Buffett as your investment consultant? Well, God is a better mentor than all these experts combined. He wants to guide you to greatness in every area of your life.

What does God's blessing look like in your life? Your kids receive better grades in school. Your car gets better gas mileage and requires fewer repairs. Your house goes up in value. You have favor with your boss at work and receive bonuses and raises. Your employees respect you. Your spouse is warm and loving. Your dog obeys your commands. You never need to go to the doctor. Your grass is always green. You win call-in radio contests. The policeman gives you a warning instead of a ticket. Your bank accounts are never overdrawn and your credit card bills are paid off monthly. You get promoted. God opens doors for you. Your investments flourish. You sleep peacefully every night. Your friends take you out for dinner at the nicest restaurants. Your clothes last longer. You are happy and content. Your appliances do not break down. You live a stress-free life. In short, the blessing of God enhances every area of your everyday life.

What Does the Word "Blessing" Mean?

Throughout the Bible, we see how important blessing is to God. In the NIV Bible, the word "bless" is found 95 times, "blessed" is found 234 times, and "blessing" is used 65 times. The Hebrew word for blessing is *barak* which means "to give abundant and effective life to someone." The Greek word for "blessing" is *eulogia* which is a combination of two words, a prefix *eu* which means "well" and *logos* which means "words." So the Greek translation could mean "well-spoken of" or "someone whom everyone speaks well of."

Blessing implies fertility of animals, abundance of crops, and many children. It means peace with those around you, security from enemies, good fortune, long life, and well-being in every area of life which includes mental and emotional health, spiritual salvation, material wealth, and physical healing.

Blessing encompasses being set free from unprofitable work, anxiousness about the future, and dependence upon another for your livelihood. Blessed people can expect a quiet life, success, supernatural protection, harmony with neighbors, victory over enemies, perpetual prosperity, family unity, and abundant provision.

Perhaps the best way to define blessing is to quote Jesus, *"...I have come that they may have life, and that they may have it more abundantly"* (John 10:10 NKJV). God does not want you to live a mediocre, substandard life of being sick and poor. God wants you to be healthy, wealthy, and wise.

According to the Bible, blessings can only come from God. The blessing of God was originally given to Abraham and today extends to all believers. It is an everlasting promise.

How Can You Be Blessed?

Do you want to be blessed? How would you like to get along better with your spouse? Have enough money in your bank account to pay your bills? Raise kids who stay out of trouble? Be promoted by your boss at work? Find a good deal when you buy a new car?

Blessing is a matter of choice, not chance. When you invite God to come live in your house, get ready, because something special is going to occur. God's presence brings God's blessing.

Life with God just keeps getting better and better. The Bible says, *"The path of the righteous is like the first gleam of dawn, shining ever brighter till the full light of day"* (Proverbs 4:18). The Apostle Paul explained that the believer should advance from *"glory to glory"* (2 Corinthians 3:18 NKJV). This means that wherever you are in your life, God has a greater level of blessing in store for you!

You may be surprised when I say that God wants to bless you. For many years, some in the church have focused more on God's judgment than on God's desire to bless His people. But I believe we should focus more on God's blessing than on His need for justice. In the next few pages, I will explain how to activate that blessing in your life.

Think Outside the Box

God wants to bless you, not punish you. In the movie "Indiana Jones and the Raiders of the Lost Ark," the evil Nazis hoped the ark would become a valuable talisman that would guarantee the success of their battle plans; instead, they all died when the holy box was opened. The inspiration for that fictional movie is the story of Uzzah who was killed when he touched the ark. For Uzzah, the ark was deadly, but for Obed-Edom it became a blessing.

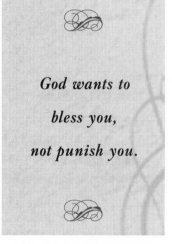

God wants to bless you, not punish you.

The question really bothered me until I saw the truth. What was the difference between Obed-Edom and Uzzah? Obed-Edom received a blessing because the ark was in his house, but Uzzah fell over dead when he touched the ark. Same ark, different results. Why was one person blessed, and the other person punished? I decided to study more about the ark. Hidden within God's instructions to Moses on how to build the ark, I discovered the answer to my question.

The ark was the Jewish people's most cherished possession because it carried the tangible presence of God on earth. It represented two things that must always be kept in balance: God's holiness and God's mercy.

The ark was basically a box built of acacia wood, overlaid with gold. According to Exodus 25:10, the ark was approximately 3.75 feet long,

2.25 feet wide, 2.25 feet high. Hidden within the box were the Ten Commandments, which are a symbol of God's law.

God's law is a manifestation of God's character of holiness. Because God loves righteousness, holiness, and truth, the law is perfect, holy, and just. All who break the law must be judged. The Old Testament is full of the law and its lists of do's and don'ts. These laws were given, not to condemn mankind, but to reveal the holy nature of God. Unfortunately, no human can live up to the demands of the law. When a human breaks one of God's laws, this is called sin.

God wants to bless you, but He cannot bless sin. Sin must be punished because the law has been broken. God's holy character demands justice. This is why Uzzah died, because he disobeyed the law by touching the ark.

God's mercy is just as big as God's judgment!

But, the cover of the box reveals a second element of God's character. Moses received God's instructions, *"...make the Ark's cover— the place of atonement—out of pure gold. It must be 3 ¾ feet long and 2 ¼ feet wide"* (Exodus 25:17 NLT). This lid is known as the "Place of Atonement" or "The Mercy Seat." Notice, the mercy seat is exactly the same size as the ark. God's mercy is just as big as God's judgment!

During Old Testament times, once each year, the high priest poured the blood of a goat over the mercy seat (Leviticus 16:15). This goat represented all the people of Israel, and in a ceremony, the sins of Israel were symbolically placed on the goat. Then the goat was killed as a sacrifice for the sins of the people. But the goat's sacrifice was temporary. Every year the death of another goat was needed.

But, God wanted to permanently remove our sins so He sent Jesus Christ, the perfect sacrifice, to die once and for all for the sins of humankind (Hebrews 9:28). When Jesus died on the cross, He paid the price for your sin and my sin. Christ's death and resurrection are evidence of God's mercy. So, in the New Testament, we discover the mercy seat.

Now for the best news of all. God says to you, *"I will meet with you, and I will speak with you from above the mercy seat..."* (Exodus 25:22 NKJV). God wants to speak to you, not where the law is kept, not where judgment is meted out, but above the mercy seat. God meets you, not in a place of judgment, but in a place of mercy! Obed-Edom was blessed because he experienced the mercy of God.

Inside the box there is judgment. But, the cover is exactly the same size as the box. God's need for judgment is completely covered by God's mercy. Outside the box, Jesus poured His blood on the mercy seat of heaven so that all can be saved.

Many preachers stay inside the box. They preach from a place of judgment and condemnation. People become depressed trying to follow an endless list of religious rules. But, God wants us to think outside the box.

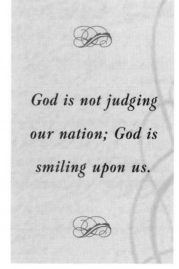

God is not judging our nation; God is smiling upon us.

I have heard preachers say that God is judging different nations. They cite terrorist attacks, hurricanes, and tsunamis as evidence. But I believe that all of God's need for judgment was poured out on Jesus at the cross. God is not judging our nation; God is smiling upon us.

Preachers, listen to me. God is not inside the box. He is waiting to meet us at the place of mercy, of forgiveness, and of love. We should preach mercy, not law.

Without the law, there is no need for grace. But, wherever the law is found, we find the law being broken and it quickly becomes obvious that grace and mercy are desperately needed. *"The law was added so that the trespass might increase. But where sin increased, grace increased all the more"* (Romans 5:20).

Without mercy, no human being could go to heaven. If we only had the law, we would be like Uzzah who died when he touched the ark. If we try to approach God from inside the box (on the basis of the law), we would be judged and condemned to an eternity separated from God. But, God does not meet us at the law (the Ten Commandments), He meets us at the mercy seat, the place of atonement and of forgiveness. God's mercy is much greater than God's need for judgment. *"Mercy triumphs over judgment!"* (James 2:13).

This is the difference between religion and a relationship with God. Religion tries to force people to stay inside the box. Religion provides a list of rules and regulations. Religion is about the law. If you try to approach God through religion, it will feel as dead as Uzzah.

But, Obed-Edom developed a relationship with God. God's presence filled his house. You can experience a similar relationship with God, not based on rules, but based on love. You do not have to serve a dead religion; you can have a relationship with a living God and be blessed, just like Obed-Edom

Jesus Thought Outside the Box

Jesus told a parable about two men who went to the temple to pray (Luke 18:9-14). One was a Pharisee, a religious leader. The second was a tax collector. The Pharisee began to pray, "God, I thank You that I am not like other men—robbers, evildoers, adulterers, or even like this tax collector. I fast twice a week and give a tenth of all I have."

But the tax collector stood in the corner. He would not even look up to heaven, but beat his breast and said, "God, have mercy on me, a sinner." Jesus said, "I tell you that the tax collector, rather than the Pharisee, went home justified before God."

The Pharisee approached God from within the BOX (based on LAW) but the tax collector approached God at the place of mercy. The tax collector was the one made righteous.

Again, in the case of the adulterous woman, the religious leaders wanted to judge her according to the law, but Jesus met her with mercy (John 8:3-11).

Before we were saved we were dead in sin. *"But because of his great love for us, God, who is rich in mercy, made us alive with Christ even when we were dead in transgressions..."* (Ephesians 2:4-5). When you die, what do they bury you in? A box. A coffin. But Jesus through His mercy made us alive. He set us free from the box. We must think outside the box!

God's Presence Gives Us Power to Live a Holy Life

The presence of God had a profound effect on Obed-Edom's life. I think that during the three months God was living in his house, Obed-Edom stopped sinning.

When I was a kid, the most hectic time in our house was when my mother received a phone call from a friend who was coming to visit. She called the whole family together and we did a five-minute cleanup. We washed the dishes, swept the floor, dusted the living room, threw our toys under the bed, folded the laundry, and straightened the pictures on the wall, all in five minutes. My mother wanted the house to be clean for her friends.

This is what I imagine happened in Obed-Edom's house. It is not every day the Creator of the Universe comes for a visit. Obed-Edom and his entire family probably cleaned up their act. They stopped willfully sinning. After all, the last person who had disobeyed the law fell over dead when he touched the ark.

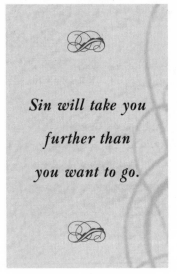

Sin will take you further than you want to go.

Sin will take you further than you want to go. It will keep you longer than you want to stay and charge you more than you want to pay. Sin won't ask for much in the beginning, but in the end, it will steal everything you have.

God's presence will help us stop sinning. If we truly understand that God is with us at all times, we will not want to do anything that could break His heart.

A car cuts you off in the middle of traffic. You curse at the driver until you glance to your right and see God sitting in your passenger seat. He says, "Why are you yelling at one of My children?"

You check your e-mail. One is from a pornographic website and in a moment of weakness you are tempted to take a peek. Just then, Jesus walks in the room and asks, "Hey, what are you looking at?"

You want to share a juicy tidbit of gossip with a friend. Jesus sees you whispering, and comes to sit beside you. When He hears what you are saying, He says, "What are you saying about My sister?"

God's presence gives us the power to live a holy life. He is the ultimate accountability partner.

God is blessing Obed-Edom. But guess what? His story is not finished yet!

CHAPTER 3

ERASING THE PAST

"…Obed-Edom of Gath."

(1 CHRONICLES 13:13 NLT)

Why me? pondered Obed-Edom. For two months now the presence of God had dwelt in his house. He was overwhelmingly grateful as he contemplated all that had happened since that fateful afternoon the ark was placed in his living room.

Previously, he had been in debt up to his eyeballs; now his treasure chest was overflowing with silver and even gold coins. He and his wife had frequently argued over absurd things; now they were best friends again. The harvest had often been poor or an outright failure; now he would reap a bumper crop. The herds were healthy and multiplying rapidly. He hired three new employees to help run his numerous business ventures. Shemaiah was finally on the honor roll at school.

Best of all, Obed-Edom had entered into a relationship with God. His daily prayer times were so real. God's presence was so strong. Every day he spoke with God and to his surprise, God spoke back to him.

Obed-Edom wondered, *Why am I so blessed? Of all the people in Israel, why did God choose to live in my house? Surely there are better candidates for God's blessing.*

The reason Obed-Edom was confused about God choosing to bless him was because of his dubious past. Obed-Edom came from a strange family background. On his father's side he was a Levite of the family of Korah in the clan of Kohath. Because he was a Levite, he was allowed by the Law of Moses to care for the ark. But the meaning of his name reveals that he was not exactly kosher.

"God, do You even know what my name means?" he prayed. Names are so important because they reveal the history and the character of a man.

"My first name, Obed, means 'slave.'" Deep inside his heart, Obed-Edom heard the voice of God gently speaking to him, "My son, you are no longer a slave."

"My second name, Edom, means I am descended from the Edomites. The Edomites are the children of Esau, the brother of Jacob. Historically, the Israelites and the Edomites have been enemies. That makes me an enemy of Israel, God." Obed-Edom thought for a moment and said, "If I am an enemy of Israel, then I am Your enemy too. How could You even allow me to care for the ark? God, how can You even trust me?"

Again God softly replied, "Son, you are not My enemy."

Obed-Edom continued as if this was a one-way conversation. "To make matters even worse, I am from the city of Gath. King David's greatest enemy, Goliath the giant, was from my home-town of Gath. How can You bless me when I was born in such a sinful city?"

God spoke one more time, "My friend, I do not care where you are from, all I care about is where you are going. Your past does not matter, I have a wonderful future for you." Obed-Edom fell silent, basking in God's presence surrounded by a cloud of incredible love and acceptance.

Just then Shemaiah ran into the living room and jumped into his father's arms asking a million questions. He knew this was the time of day his father finished praying and he asked at lightning speed. "Father, what did God tell you today? What has happened in the fields? Oh, I forgot to tell you, I was the best student in class today. What have you learned about God? How long will the ark be here? Can we keep it?"

"Slow down, Shem, I cannot possibly answer all those questions right now, but I will tell you what I have learned today. God has shared with me that I am His friend."

"Wow!" Shemaiah shouted, "God is your best friend!"

"Yes. I can also tell you that He loves us all. It doesn't matter where we came from or what people say about us, God knows us and loves us."

"What about King David, Father? Does God know him too?"

"Yes, Shem, God loves King David very much. Enough questions. Hurry now and finish your chores. It's almost dinnertime."

Leave Your Past Behind You

Has anyone ever labeled you? A label is like an ugly internal tattoo. I have a friend who was teased in grade school by bullies. They called her a variety of negative names like "Four-Eyes," "Stupid," "Dummy," and "Fatty." For years my friend was haunted by these mean words. The negative labels shaped her image of herself, which was sad, because as an adult she was both good-looking and smart. She allowed the opinion of others to destroy her potential.

Obed-Edom was also labeled. The Bible does not tell us much about his background, but I did discover some clues when I looked up the meaning of his name in a Bible dictionary.

His first name "Obed" means "servant or slave." Obed-Edom was stuck in a box that labeled him as a slave.

His second name "Edom" means he was descended from the Edomites who were enemies of Israel. The Edomites were decended from Esau (the brother of Jacob). Edom was the land southeast of Palestine. The word "Edom" actually means "red" because Esau had a head of fiery red hair. His nickname was "Edom" or "Red."

David conquered the land of Edom and all the Edomites became his servants. *"David became famous after he returned from striking down eighteen thousand Edomites…"* (2 Samuel 8:13). *"And he put garrisons in Edom…and all they of Edom became David's servants…"* (2 Samuel 8:14 KJV). So Obed-Edom was known as "the slave who is the enemy of Israel."

Then, to top it all off, the Bible tells us that Obed-Edom was from the city of Gath which was bad news because Goliath the giant, David's greatest enemy, was from the city of Gath.

Every time people called Obed-Edom's name they were reinforcing a negative image. People would literally shout at him "Hey, slave." Can you imagine being stuck with that horrible name? He had the equivalent of "born to lose" tattooed on his soul.

Obed-Edom had three strikes against him. He was a slave, he was an enemy of Israel, and he grew up in the wrong city. People had labeled him. He was a nobody. He came from a disadvantaged background. He grew up in the wrong neighborhood. He was poor. His people had been disenfranchised. Of all the people in Israel, he seemed the least likely for God to bless.

You may feel like Obed-Edom.

- Was your family poor?
- Did you grow up on the wrong side of the tracks?
- Do you come from an unpleasant family background?
- Did you ever drop out of school?
- Have you made any mistakes in your life?
- Are you stuck in a dead-end, low-paying job?
- Have you ever been passed up for a promotion at work?
- Have people labeled you and called you horrible names?
- Did you feel unloved and rejected as a young child?
- Did you come from a dysfunctional home?
- Were you ignored and ridiculed in school?

- Have you ever been physically abused?

- Are you so wounded from the past that it is difficult for you to form normal relationships?

- Did kids at school ever call you names?

- Did you grow up with a poor self-image?

- Have you ever struggled with an inferiority complex?

- Are you dissatisfied with your physical appearance?

- Have people teased you because you are too fat, too thin, or too short?

- Does your spouse treat you poorly?

- Has anyone ever discriminated against you?

- Have you ever felt like a loser?

All these circumstances can cause pain, but I want you to know:

- It does not matter who you are.

- It does not matter where you are from.

- It does not matter what your occupation is.

- It does not matter what your IQ is.

- It does not matter what your economic status is.

- It does not matter how much education you have.

- It does not matter what your skin color is.

- It does not matter what country you are from.

- It does not matter who you know.

- It does not matter what your family history is.

When God Moves in, You're Blessed!

God never judges your past to decide your future.

The life of Obed-Edom reveals incredible truth. God never judges your past to decide your future. Always look through the windshield of life, not the rearview mirror. An ordinary person can accomplish extraordinary things! God can turn a nobody into a somebody!

When you become a follower of Jesus Christ, you become a new creation. The old is gone, the new has come. Everything negative about your past is washed away. Your past sin, past failures, past disappointments, and past offenses are gone. You are given a brand-new start. You are like a butterfly that starts life as an ugly caterpillar. Caterpillars crawl on the ground. But then they spin a cocoon and when they push their way free, they look completely different. They become a beautiful butterfly that can soar up into the sky!

God has given Obed-Edom a brand-new start, but guess what? His story is not finished yet.

CHAPTER 4

ADDICTED TO GOD'S PRESENCE

King David was told, "The LORD has blessed the household of Obed-Edom and everything he has, because of the ark of God." So David went down and brought up the ark of God from the house of Obed-Edom to the City of David with rejoicing.

(2 SAMUEL 6:12)

King David yawned in the heat of the sultry afternoon as he sat under the palace portico overlooking the city of Jerusalem. Flies buzzed lazily about while a servant absently waved a fan to keep them from landing on platters overflowing with assorted fruit. A palace courtier nodded and stood before the king holding a scroll, and began to read in a drone from a scroll of current events in Israel.

"What's happening of note in my kingdom?" interrupted King David.

"My liege, do you remember the man, Obed-Edom?"

"No, who is he?"

"Remember? You left the Ark of the Covenant in his house," prompted the reader.

"Don't remind me of that. Trying to bring the ark to Jerusalem was a public relations fiasco," complained the king.

"Well, you should hear what people are saying about this man, Obed-Edom."

"What do you mean? What happened? Did he die? Did he touch the ark too? Is he complaining about storing the ark?"

"No, your majesty, God is blessing his house!"

The king leaned forward. "He's being blessed?"

"Yes, sir, he and his entire household! His family is blessed. His marriage is blessed. His children are blessed. His crops are blessed. His animals are blessed. His business is blessed. Everything he touches prospers!"

"Hmm. How long has the ark been in his house?" queried King David.

"Three months," answered the courtier after consulting his scroll.

"And you say he's been blessed ever since God's presence entered his house?"

"Yes, my king."

"That is amazing!' the king said excitedly, "we need the entire nation of Israel to be blessed. Hurry, call my advisors. Let's bring the ark to Jerusalem as quickly as possible."

When the king's royal guard rode down the road from Jerusalem, Shemaiah was the first to spot them, riding hard and fast in a cloud of dust. He ran to tell his father about the commotion.

A sinking feeling filled the pit of Obed-Edom's stomach. He left the lamb he was shearing and ran to the front of the house, calling his entire family to join him.

The entourage from Jerusalem quickly halted in front of Obed-Edom's house. A white stallion reared up, snorting as it came to a standstill on the doorstep. King David dismounted, bellowing to a rider behind him, "Is this the man who has been blessed?"

"He is, my liege."

Obed-Edom dropped to one knee. "Gracious king, may God bless you and Israel with life, prosperity, and health all the days of your life. My family and I are honored to have you visit us."

"I have come for the ark. You have done well in keeping it safe and I am grateful that it rested in the home of a worthy man. But now I must return to Jerusalem with the ark so that the nation of Israel can be as blessed as you have been."

"No," pleaded Shemaiah, peeking from behind his father. "No!"

"Hush, Shem, we must not keep what belongs to all of Israel. God wants to bless the whole nation. He just chose us to take care of the ark until He was ready to take it to Jerusalem."

"But, father, I like the ark in our home."

"Shemaiah, don't worry," soothed Obed-Edom, but inside his heart he was sorrowful too.

King David brought the ark to Jerusalem that same afternoon. This time, four Levites slowly carried the ark on their shoulders using wooden poles. The entire nation celebrated as the ark entered the gates of Jerusalem with great fanfare. King David rejoiced like never before.

Only Obed-Edom was sad. The last three months had been so amazing; he had hoped the ark would stay in his house forever. Obed-Edom realized he had become addicted to God's presence.

He had come to love the prayer times, the unity in his family, and the way the true and living God had become his friend.

Because of the blessing he received he understood better than anyone why King David wanted so desperately to bring the Ark of the Covenant back to its rightful resting place. During his prayer times Obed-Edom had come to know the heart of God. God desired to dwell among all His people.

As he watched the Ark of the Covenant being removed from his home he asked himself, *What can I do to stay close to the presence of God?*

Are You Addicted?

In ninety short days God's presence in his home had radically changed Obed-Edom's life. Obed-Edom became so addicted to God's presence that he followed the ark to Jerusalem. He was willing to do whatever it took to stay close to God's presence.

Addiction is when you cannot live without something, when you have a compulsion, a craving, an obsession, a need, a strong desire, an inability to do without, to develop a dependency, when you want something above all else. We often think of addiction as negative, but addiction can be positive too. It all depends on what or who you are addicted to.

People addicted to drugs desperately look for their next fix, but people who are addicted to God also get a fix, a fix to all their problems. God is the ultimate fix. He will fix your marriage, your attitudes, your problems, your body, your finances, etc. A drug addict cannot wait for another fix and will do anything for a high. When we become addicted to God's presence we are also willing to do whatever it takes to be close to Him.

Have you ever held your breath under water? For the first thirty seconds you feel fine. But then your heart starts beating faster, your veins crave more oxygen, your lungs scream for air, and finally your body kicks its way to the surface of the water. With deep gulps, you gasp for air. In those moments right before your brain blacks out, you are willing to do anything for one more breath. This desperation is what an addiction to God's presence is like. We should desire God's presence as much as we desire to breathe.

You can have a tangible sense of God's presence in your life. *"For in him we live and move and have our being…"* (Acts 17:28). It's true. Apart from God, there is no existence, no meaning, no purpose for living, no hope, and no success.

God's presence changes your life forever; your motives, your priorities, and your focus. His will becomes your will. God's presence becomes life itself.

As a human being, you were created to worship. You will worship something. The question is: What will you worship? Money? Sex? Power? Your spouse? Your kids? Ministry? Achievement? Shopping? Sports? A celebrity? Your church? What you worship is revealed by what you focus on.

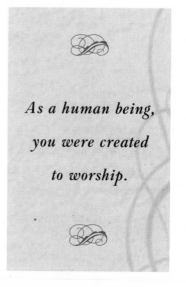

As a human being, you were created to worship.

Even ministers need be to reminded to focus more on God and less on the ministry. Sam Hinn says, "You are called into ministry, but you were created to worship." Worship is who I am, ministry is what I do. Who you are is a worshiper; what you do is the work. Mike Bickle adds, "God wants us to be something, before He wants us to do something." What we do should flow out of who we are. The fact that we are seeking His presence is far more important to God than the fact that we are involved in the ministry. Our ministry to others should flow from our time in God's presence.

Four Keys to Staying in God's Presence

The presence of God is the greatest commodity in the universe, but how do we stay in God's presence? How can we become addicted to God's presence the way Obed-Edom was?

1. Read the Bible.

The Bible is God's Word for your life. Just as the physical body needs nourishment from food, your spiritual life needs nourishment from the Word of God. Through the Bible, God speaks to your heart and reveals His plan for your life. As you study the Scriptures you will grow closer to God's presence.

The Bible is God's love letter to you. Contained in this book are God's laws for living, the history of God's dealings with humans, wonderful psalms and proverbs, prophetic warnings and encouragement, the life of Jesus, an explanation of Christian doctrine, and a look at the future when Jesus returns as a reigning King. It is a living and powerful book.

2. Pray.

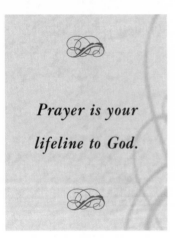

Prayer is your lifeline to God.

Prayer is your lifeline to God. When you do not feel the presence of God, He has not moved, you have. Prayer is simply talking to God from your heart. Tell God what you are feeling and let Him know what you are going through. God wants you to take your problems to Him because He is interested in helping you in every area of your life. Thank Him for His goodness in your life. Tell Him how much you love Him.

Prayer is a two-way conversation. *"Call to me and I will answer you and tell you great...things you do not know"* (Jeremiah 33:3). Not only does it involve talking to God, but also being quiet and listening to Him talk to you. A radio station is continually broadcasting, but unless you tune your radio to the proper frequency you will not pick up the signal. In the same way, you will find that God is always willing to talk with you, but you must be tuned into what He is saying by spending time praying.

3. Fellowship with others who are addicted to His presence.

One twig can be easily broken, but many branches tied together are impossible to break. We need to go to church in order to gain strength from other believers. It is impossible to be a strong Christian by yourself. The Bible reminds us, *"Let us not give up meeting together, as some are in the habit of doing, but let us encourage one another—and all the more as you see the Day approaching"* (Hebrews 10:25). As the time comes closer for Jesus to return, it is even more vitally important for us to fellowship with other believers in a church Body, which is the visible manifestation of God's Kingdom on earth.

As you grow in the Lord, you'll need support, encouragement, and training from other believers. This means you need to belong to a church. If you are not already a member of a church, find one where the Word of God is faithfully proclaimed and the presence of God is celebrated. A place where people are being saved and healed and you can have relationship with other members of the Body of Christ.

Look for opportunities to serve in your church. If you are continually being fed without having a place to give to others, you will become spiritually bloated. Finding a place to serve is an important way for you to guarantee that you stay hungry for God. Obed-Edom became addicted to God's presence when God was living in his house, but as you will see in the coming chapters, he fed his addiction as he served in the house of God.

4. Stay close to Jesus.

"You be the crab. I'll be the fish," my wife mumbled in her sleep one night. That was a weird thing for her to say to me, so allow me to explain our private joke.

On our honeymoon in Hawaii we watched an Imax-theater movie about the coral reefs of the South Pacific. The most memorable part of the documentary involved a symbiotic relationship between a certain type of crab and a fish. The crab dug a hole in the sand and the fish used the hole to hide from predators. The fish would float next to the hole keeping an eye out for enemies while the crab pushed rocks around making the hole bigger. As the crab dug, he always kept one long antenna on the fish. No matter how hard he worked, his feeler would be touching the fish. As soon as the fish sensed an enemy and ducked back in the hole, the crab would feel the movement and have time to scurry to safety.

My wife was sleepily asking me to touch some part of her lightly as we slept. My big toe, or a finger, or an arm draped over her to let her know I was still in bed and not off typing on my computer in the middle of the night. She wanted to know I was present even when she was sleeping.

In our relationship with Jesus, we should be like the crab. As we go about our daily work, we should keep one of our feelers on Jesus to find out what He is doing. We may be busy, but we can stay aware of His presence. Not only will this protect us from danger, it will also enhance our work and increase our sensitivity to what God is doing.

Obed-Edom's story could have ended when David removed the ark from his house, but guess what? His story is not finished yet.

CHAPTER 5

SERVING THE HOUSE OF GOD

"So the Levites appointed...Obed-Edom...
[to be a gatekeeper]."

(1 CHRONICLES 15:17-18)

"Honey, I want to follow the Ark of the Covenant to Jerusalem," Obed-Edom said to his wife. "In the last three months while the ark has been in our house, I have become addicted to the presence of God. I need to do whatever it takes to stay close to God."

"But what about the new businesses you started?" worried his wife. "Who will bring in the harvest? Who will help me with the kids?"

"Don't worry, sweetheart. The Lord will help us take care of all of that as we follow Him," Obed-Edom said. "All I know is that I need to stay close to God's presence. We've never experienced blessings like we have in the last three months. Give me some time in Jerusalem to make arrangements for you and our family and then I will send for you and the kids."

Obed-Edom tearfully hugged his family good-bye. He then hastily grabbed his travel bag and walked out the door taking his first steps as a pilgrim towards Jerusalem.

As he entered the capital city, he gazed in awe at its massive protective walls and the busy multitudes going about their daily trade and commerce. With eager determination, he made his way over to the new tabernacle where the ark was now kept.

Before He could scarcely even wonder, *What do I do now, Lord?* he overheard a conversation between two temple priests who came and stood next to him.

As they exchanged concerned glances with each other, Obed-Edom heard one of them say, "You know, we are a little short-handed and need volunteers to guard the temple gates. Do you know of anyone who would be willing to help us out?"

Obed-Edom cleared his throat and bravely stepped forward, "Hello, sirs, and excuse me for interrupting, but I couldn't help but overhear your conversation. My name is Obed-Edom and I'm willing to help."

The priests stared at him skeptically. "Aren't you Obed-Edom, the slave? You're an enemy of Israel from the city of Gath. What makes you think you can be a temple guard?"

"The ark was in my house for three months and God's presence changed my life," Obed-Edom hastily explained. "I'll do whatever I can to serve God."

One of the priests eyed Obed-Edom warily, his hands on his hips, unconvinced of his sincerity. "This is a very difficult job. You'd be the first one up in the morning to open the temple gates. You'd have to stand next to the gates all day in the hot sun and be the last to leave in the evening. What makes you think you can do it?"

"Sir. I know I can if you'll just give me the opportunity. Since God has blessed my house, I'll do whatever I can to bless His house."

"Well, it's not like we have a whole lot of choice right now," said the other priest with resignation in his voice. "All right, then. We'll start you as a novice gatekeeper."

Over the next few weeks Obed-Edom was determined to be the best gatekeeper in the temple. He woke before sunrise every day and made his way through still sleepy streets to open the bulky temple gates. All day long he welcomed people warmly as they arrived with children and animals in tow to worship at the temple. He quickly became known as the friendliest gatekeeper. He shared his brief testimony with as many people as would listen.

"Did you hear that the ark was in my house for three months?" he would ask anyone who cared to listen. "During those three months, I was blessed. My family, my marriage, my business, and my crops were blessed. As a matter of fact, I am still being blessed. As you worship God in the temple, you can expect God to bless you too!"

"Thank you for your kindness and keeping the ark safe for us," one pilgrim said. "Do you still spend time with God like you did when the ark was in your house?"

"Oh yes, that is the best part of my day," Obed-Edom replied eagerly. " I find myself in prayer and worship all day long. This has been the best experience of my life."

Obed-Edom was blessed being a doorkeeper for the Lord. He desired to be the best because he had been given the best.

At sunset, when the day was finished, Obed-Edom was always the last gatekeeper to leave the temple. He'd sweep up the litter in the entrance and polish the brass gates before locking them up for the night watch. Many times as he strode to his lodging, he would take one long look in the direction of the ark and say in his heart to himself, *I'll be here bright and early in the morning, Lord. You can count on me. Thank You for blessing me.* Because God had blessed his house, Obed-Edom was eager to take every opportunity to bless God's house.

I can see I'll be here awhile. I think it's time for my family to make Jerusalem their new home!

The Link Between Your House and God's House

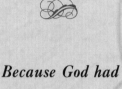

Because God had blessed his house, he decided to bless God's house.

Obed-Edom discovered an important principle. Because God had blessed his house, he decided to bless God's house. The success of God's house and the success of your house are intertwined. As God blesses your house, you can bless God's house and as God's house is blessed, your house will be blessed.

Obed-Edom became a gatekeeper in the house of God. What were his duties? Well, he helped collect the offerings (2 Kings 22:4). He guarded the entrance to the temple (1 Chronicles 9:19), and he probably greeted people as they arrived at the temple.

Obed-Edom's serving as a gatekeeper reminds me of another gatekeeper I know. At my home church, there is an older gentleman who greets people as they arrive on Sunday morning. He always has a huge smile and shakes my hand as I enter the building. For over twenty years, he has volunteered as a greeter. He found a way to serve God and has remained faithfully at his post. Because of his faithfulness, God has blessed him!

Every person who volunteers in the house of God can expect to be blessed. Every seed you sow into the Kingdom of God produces a harvest of blessing in your life. In what ways are you a blessing in the house of God?

Are you a greeter in your local church? An usher? Do you volunteer to work with the children? Have you ever helped in the nursery? Do you teach a Sunday school class? Are you an altar counselor? Do you play an instrument in the worship group? Do you lead a small group? Do you help clean the church? Do you visit people in the hospital or in jail? Are you part of a prayer chain? Do you mentor a teenager in the things of God? Do you serve on an advisory board? Are you a deacon, an elder, a pastor, or a bishop? Have you ever gone on a mission trip? Have you given away a gospel tract or witnessed to someone?

If you have found a place to serve in the house of God, you can expect God's blessings to pour down upon your life. There is a place for you to serve in your church. The purpose of church is not just to sit and listen to the preacher preach. It is vital to be involved, to be a part of what God is doing. We should be able to say along with King David, *"Zeal for your house consumes me..."* (Psalm 69:9).

If you are willing to be used by God, there is a place for you to serve in His Kingdom. Traditionally there has been a separation between the clergy and the laity. The professional clergy (pastors, reverends, missionaries) did the ministry and the laity (church members) sat in the pews. When I hear the word "laity," I don't imagine them sitting in the pews so much as laying down in the pews. But every believer is called to be a minister. There is something you can do to help your local church.

God wants every church member to be a minister. Not everyone can preach, but everyone can do something to be a blessing to the house of God. You might have never imagined yourself as a minister, but this may be because you had the wrong idea of what ministry is. Ministry is not just preaching. Ministry can be picking up a paint brush and painting the children's rooms at church, taking a bag of groceries to a shut-in, praying for a family member, or singing in the choir. There are as many potential ministries in the church as there are people in the church.

You may not be called to minister from a stage, but there is an area where you can serve. When you find your place to serve, you activate the blessing of Obed-Edom in your life.

A Lesson from Haggai

The short book of Haggai reveals the connection between God's house and your house. In the beginning of the book, we learn that the people of Israel were neglecting God's house in order to focus on their own houses. The Lord asks through the prophet Haggai, *"Is it a time for you to be living in your paneled houses while God's house remains a ruin?"* (Haggai 1:4).

Then Haggai reminds God's people about all the bad things that are happening as a result of them neglecting God's house. They work hard but do not make much money. Food, drink, and clothing are scarce. The money they earn falls out of holes in the bottom of their purses. They are like a car with spinning wheels. The engine is racing but the car is going nowhere.

The people repented because of Haggai's preaching and began to work on the house of God. Three months later, their situation was turned around. God promises, *"From this day on I will bless you"* (Haggai 2:19). The end of the story is found in Ezra 6:14: *"So the elders of the Jews continued to build and prosper under the preaching of Haggai the prophet...."*

As they continued to build, they prospered. Working part-time building God's house and part-time running their own businesses gave them more profit than they had when working full time for themselves. Why?

They activated God's blessing upon their lives. You and God partnering together takes you much further than you working by yourself.

With Great Blessing Comes Great Responsibility

When I was a kid, my parents required me to perform daily chores. I loaded the dishwasher, gathered the laundry, washed the car, and dusted the living room. Often I complained to my mom, "Why do I have to do chores?" Her answer was always the same, "Because you live here. You want to eat, don't you?" Along with the privilege of eating my mother's cooking came the responsibility of doing chores.

God's house is the same. Along with the blessing of God comes an opportunity to serve. We are servants. A servant is usually clothed by his master, given a place to sleep, and fed. But the blessing of free clothes, housing, and food carries with it the responsibility of completing a duty. Many desire the blessing of God, but few are willing to pay the price.

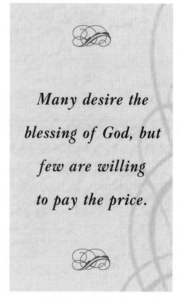

Many desire the blessing of God, but few are willing to pay the price.

In today's busy society with kids' soccer games, two parents working, school activities, business meetings, and must-see TV, some people say they cannot afford to spend time serving at church. But, if it is true that the success of your house and the success of God's house are linked, then you cannot afford not to find a way to bless God's house. Serving is more than an obligation; it is a privilege.

What opportunities are available in your church to serve God? Have you thought about volunteering in any of these areas?

- Usher
- Greeter
- Children's worker
- Parking lot attendant
- Youth ministry
- Musician
- Choir singer
- Office assistant
- Call people to pray with them
- Hospital visitation
- Church setup or takedown crew
- Sound system technician
- Take food to elderly shut-ins
- Nursery volunteer
- Help clean the church
- Tell your friends about Jesus
- Bus driver to give rides to church
- Invite your next-door neighbor to church
- Host a home Bible study
- Go on a mission trip
- Drama or dance team
- Altar call counselor
- Armor bearer for your pastor
- Hand out invitations to your church in your community

Obed-Edom started being blessed when God came to live in his house, but as we will discover in the rest of this book, he continued to be blessed because he served in God's house. When you neglect God's house, you turn off the flow of God's blessing. But, when you bless God's house, you invite God's blessing upon your own house. As God's Word says, *"Those who are planted in the house of the Lord shall flourish…"* (Psalm 92:13 NKJV).

Perhaps Obed-Edom was the inspiration for the song written by the sons of Korah. They sang, *"How lovely is your dwelling place, O LORD Almighty!"* (Psalm 84:1), and they continued, *"Blessed are those who dwell in your house; they are ever praising you"* (Psalm 84:4). Then they sang their greatest revelation of all, *"Better is one day in your courts than a thousand elsewhere; I would rather be a doorkeeper in the house of my God than dwell in the tents of the wicked"* (Psalm 84:10). What were they saying? It is better to spend one day serving in the house of God than to spend a thousand days as the king of the world.

So, now Obed-Edom is a gatekeeper in the house of God, but guess what? His story is not finished yet.

CHAPTER 6

USING YOUR TALENTS

"...Obed-Edom...[was] to play the [harp]...."

(1 CHRONICLES 15:21)

"Today we are holding auditions for the temple worship group," announced a priest as people gathered in the courtyard. Upon hearing these words, Obed-Edom became excited. When he was a child, his mother had forced him to take harp lessons. He hadn't practiced as much as she wished, but he loved to worship God. Perhaps there was a spot for him in the band.

When he showed up to audition that weekend, his heart sank like a stone. There were dozens of other men queued with harps in hand, tuning their instruments. He could tell that many were more skilled than him. He prayed for God's anointing and when his turn came, he walked forward before the priests with confidence.

"May I sing a melody I composed myself?" he requested respectfully.

He began lightly brushing his fingertips over the harp strings, "I wrote this song during one of my morning devotion times. It is about how God's presence changed my life."

As he played a simple melody that rose and fell in rhythm, the sweet presence of God filled the room and the priests looked at one another. Obed-Edom tuned them out and closed his eyes, worshipfully playing his harp for an audience of One.

When the list of musicians was posted, his name appeared as one of the harp players appointed to worship before the Lord. Obed-Edom was thrilled! He had moved from a position outside the gates of the temple to inside the courtyard of the temple. Now he could worship God all day long.

Are You Willing?

Look at the people who made the band along with Obed-Edom. Heman, Asaph and Ethan were to sound the bronze cymbals. Zechariah, Aziel, and a bunch of other guys whose names are too difficult to pronounce were to play electric guitars. Do you know why my version of the Bible says "electric guitars"? Because I am reading from the *Amplified Version.* Get it? Then, third from last, we find Obed-Edom's name as one of the harp players.

Obed-Edom may not have been the most talented harp player in all of Israel, but he was available and willing to be used. God is not looking for mere talent, He is looking for someone who is willing. God does not call the equipped, rather He equips those whom He calls. It is not your ability that impresses God, but your availability. He is not checking your aptitude, but your attitude. God is not concerned with your credentials, but with your character. He is not excited about your position, but your disposition. God does not care about your title or talent, but your testimony.

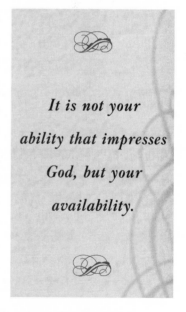

It is not your ability that impresses God, but your availability.

God is not impressed with your IQ, He is impressed with your I WILL. God needs you to say, "I WILL make a difference. I WILL serve the Kingdom of heaven. I WILL find my place of ministry in the church. I WILL be used by God." I like what Muhammad Ali, the great boxer, said, "The will must be stronger than the skill." God is looking for an army of the willing. God reduced Gideon's army from the thirty-two

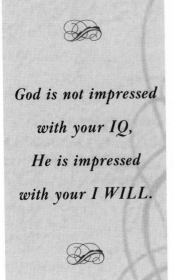

God is not impressed with your IQ, He is impressed with your I WILL.

thousand who reluctantly volunteered to only three hundred men who were genuinely willing and ready to be used.

Martin Luther King, Jr. agreed with this principle when he said, "Everybody can be great...because anybody can serve. You don't have to have a college degree to serve. You don't have to make your subject and verb agree to serve. You only need a heart full of grace. A soul generated by love."

People cry out to God saying, "Use me!" They sing the song made popular by Ron Kenoly, "Lord, if You can use anything, You can use me." Then when our pastor calls and asks for help picking kids up for Vacation Bible School, we pretend to check our calendars, hem and haw, and finally offer an excuse. Afterwards, we complain, "Pastor just wants to use me. I feel so used at this church." Do you see the dilemma? We pray to be used, but then complain when we are used. If you want to be used by God, find a place where you can meet the needs of others.

Many who volunteer complain that their load is the heaviest, but stop a moment and look at your hands. Are there any nail scars there? If there are not, then quit all that complaining. Jesus is the only one who has any right to complain and you never hear Him saying anything.

God chooses to use us. We are His voice, His hands, and His feet here on earth. God needs to use us. T. L. Osborn said, "You know if God had smarter people, He would use them, but we are all He's got."

God's never had anyone qualified working for Him yet. Abraham lied to Pharaoh that his wife was his sister, yet he is known as the "father of faith." Moses had such a temper he killed an Egyptian, yet he is the man

God chose to lead the children of Israel out of Egypt. David committed adultery with Bathsheba, and engineered the murder of her husband Uriah, yet the Bible calls him "a man after God's own heart." Elijah challenged the prophets of Baal on Mt. Carmel, called down fire from heaven, then ran scared into the desert because of the threats of Queen Jezebel. Peter cut off a servant's ear, denied Jesus three times, yet he was the disciple who preached on the Day of Pentecost.

God is glorified when we use our talents for Him. Handel's masterpiece, "The Messiah," brings glory to God every time it is sung. Michelangelo's painting on the roof of the Sistine Chapel glorifies God. Mel Gibson's movie "The Passion of the Christ" glorifies God. A four year old's finger painting of Moses crossing the Red Sea glorifies God. A grandmother baking cookies for a shut-in neighbor glorifies God. When we use our talents for God, heaven moves closer to earth.

Parable of the Talents

If you do not USE your talents, you will LOSE your talents. But when you do use your talents, you will be given more. In the Parable of the Talents in Matthew, chapter 25, Jesus tells us a story about a rich man who goes on a journey. Before he leaves, the rich man gives five talents to one servant, two talents to another servant, and one talent to a third servant. When the master returns after a long time, the first servant says, "Lord, you entrusted me with five talents. I have used it to gain five more talents." The master replies, "Well done, my good and faithful servant. You have been faithful with a few things, now I will put you in charge of many things!"

The servant with the two talents also doubled his money and was rewarded accordingly. Tragically, the servant with one talent hid his money and failed to use it wisely. When the master returned, he was angry with the servant who had wasted his resources. The lazy servant was stripped of his one talent and punished by being thrown out into darkness where there is "weeping and gnashing of teeth."

By burying the talents his master gave him, the third servant made a serious mistake. Worthless servants are not kept on the payroll for long. A worthless servant is one who does not produce. In the business world, worthless employees are fired. God's Kingdom works on a similar principle. In the Garden of Eden, God gave a mandate to mankind to multiply. God has a nature of increase, so He cannot tolerate an unproductive servant. The servant who hid his talent was not punished for adultery or for murder but for failing to use his small gift for God's Kingdom.

In Luke 19:17, we discover the faithful servant's reward is to be put in charge of ten cities. Because the servant is faithful with a small sum, he is given ten cites. His reward for faithfulness greatly outweighs his original responsibility. We see this in the story of Rebekah watering the camels in Genesis 24. Because she is willing to water the camels of an anonymous stranger, she is given the opportunity to marry the wealthiest man of her day.

The reward for work well done in God's Kingdom is "more work."

This reveals one of the greatest principles of God's Kingdom. When you are faithful with small things, God will put you in charge of many things. The reward for work well done in God's Kingdom is "more work." I do not know about you, but I want to do as much for God in my lifetime as I possibly can. I do not want to be stuck trying to do the same small things over and over again

What do we learn from the Parable of the Talents? When we are faithful with what God gives us, He will give us more. If we are unfaithful with what God gives us, we will lose even what we have.

In Matthew 21:19, Jesus cursed a fig tree that was not bearing fruit and the tree withered up and died. In heaven, there will be a "fig check" to see if you have produced any fruit with your life. At the throne of God you will be judged on the condition of your soul, but you will be rewarded based on what you accomplished with your talents, your gifts, and your abilities. Who you are is God's gift to you, what you become is your gift to God.

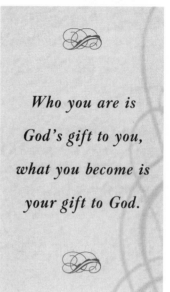

Who you are is God's gift to you, what you become is your gift to God.

In heaven there will be a reckoning. We will account for what God has given us. That concerns me a little. Am I using the abilities God gave me wisely?

After a LONG time, the master came back. It takes a while to prove yourself faithful. The unproductive servant pretended to be about his master's business, but when the reckoning came, he was found to be lacking. Do not be caught pretending when Jesus comes.

"But I don't have any special abilities," you might say to yourself. You may not be an eloquent preacher, or a beautiful singer, or a great leader, but there is something inside you that God can use. Your gifts, talents, and abilities are not your creation; they are your discovery. God gave abilities to you, and your involvement with the Kingdom causes them to surface. As you get busy for God, your gifts will be revealed. You may feel you have no talents that can be used by God. But regardless of how little talent you have, God can find a way to use you for His glory.

> *God can use literally anything you are willing to give Him.*

You may not feel you have the talent to accomplish great things, but if you are willing to be used, God is able to give you the abilities you need to complete His task. God can use literally anything you are willing to give Him.

How I Discovered My Talents

When I was a teenager I performed as a clown for birthday parties. A church heard about my show and invited me to visit their Sunday school. This opened up opportunities for me to minister to children in churches across America with my circus act. Later, these relationships with churches developed into the international traveling ministry I have today. You may not know how to juggle or create balloon animals, but you have some talent that you can give God.

God has entrusted you with something you can use for His Kingdom. God has given each of us at least one talent. You probably have more than one. Are you good at singing? Acting? Cooking? Listening? Telling stories? Raising children? Dancing? Writing? Preaching? Visiting the sick? Cleaning? Shopping? What are you good at? What do you enjoy doing? God has given you a special gift you can use for His Kingdom.

If you do not know what your talent is, try doing something until you discover your gift. When I sing I have the type of voice that scares birds away. My brother Stephen is extremely gifted musically, and my off-key singing drives him nuts. When we minister together, he strictly instructs me not to sing in the microphone, but sometimes I am so enthusiastic that I forget. Once the situation got so bad my brother told the soundman, "If Daniel starts singing, mute his microphone." Obviously I am not gifted to sing, but my singing did not bother God. He was happy that I was glorifying Him. Because of my intense desire to worship God, He was able to use me in other areas.

As you prove yourself faithful with the talents God has given you, He will increase your abilities. You will never be given more until you maximize what God has already given you. But, as you continue to serve God with all your heart, five years from now you will be amazed at what God allows you to do.

Obed-Edom is using his talents to worship in the temple band, but guess what? His story is not finished yet.

Our Goal?
Every Soul!

Daniel & Jessica King

Soulwinning Festivals

When Daniel King was fifteen years old, he set a goal to lead 1,000,000 people to Jesus before his thirtieth birthday. Instead of trying to become a millionaire, he decided to lead a million "heirs" into the Kingdom of God.

"If you belong to Christ, then you are...heirs..." (Galatians 3:29). After celebrating the completion of this goal, Daniel and Jessica made it their mission to go for one million souls every year.

This **Quest for Souls** is accomplished through:

- Soulwinning Festivals
- Leadership Training
- Literature Distribution
- Humanitarian Relief

Would you help us lead

people to Jesus by joining

The MillionHeirs' Club?

Visit www.kingministries.com to get involved!

CHAPTER 7

FAITHFULNESS IN THE HOUSE OF GOD

"…Obed-Edom…[was] also to be [a doorkeeper]
…for the ark."

(1 CHRONICLES 15:24)

Obed-Edom looked up from strumming his harp as the high priest approached him. The jeweled breastplate of the high priest glittered in the sunshine as he asked, "Obed-Edom, would you be willing to be a doorkeeper for the ark?"

Ever ready to help, Obed-Edom nodded his head although he was disappointed to be sent back to the temple gates. "After all these years, perhaps my harp playing has not improved enough," he contemplated to himself.

"Great!" exclaimed the priest, "you will be stationed directly outside the doors leading to the holy place."

"The holy place?" stuttered Obed-Edom, "but that's where the ark is kept!" Far from being disciplined, he was being promoted.

"That's right," said the priest, "we want our best worshipers to be near the presence of God."

As the priest walked away, robes swishing against the ground, Obed-Edom realized he had just been promoted to an honored position. *"Wow! I began as a gatekeeper for the temple and now I'll be a doorkeeper for the ark. I will be standing right in front of the doors leading into the Holy of Holies."*

That evening as he stood guard gazing across the temple court-yard swathed in moonlight, Obed-Edom prayed, "Dear God, when You came to live in my house, I fell in love with Your presence. Thank You for allowing me to once again be so close to Your dwelling place on earth. I want to get closer and closer to You. Amen."

Be Faithful

By this time, Obed-Edom was sure God had special plans for him. He could have been discouraged when asked to be the doorkeeper for the ark. He could have complained to himself, "Why do I have to be a doorkeeper? Can't they see that God's hand of blessing is on my life? I already spent time as a gatekeeper, now they want me to be a doorkeeper."

But, instead of complaining, Obed-Edom realized he was one step closer to the destiny God had in store for him. This was a promotion. Obed-Edom moved from the outside gate as a gatekeeper, to the courtyard as a harp player, and now he is a doorkeeper for the ark right in front of the holy place where the ark is kept. What was happening? Obed-Edom was moving closer and closer and closer to the presence of God.

God wants to do the same miracle in your life. He wants you to come closer and closer to His presence.

It seems everyone in the Body of Christ wants to be promoted. We keep looking for the next level of anointing, new revelation, more blessing, or a bigger prophecy. We run from a "double-portion" conference to a "special anointing" service to a "more than conquerors" revival. But many of these meetings seem to do little good. Christians stay stuck in the same rut they have been in for years.

Chasing more blessing is like a dog chasing his tail. He is trying to catch what he already has. You have already been given *every spiritual blessing in Christ* (Ephesians 1:3). What more could you want? We are already blessed, but there is one thing we need in order for God to promote us.

You see, promotion will never come simply because someone lays a hand on your head and pronounces you blessed. God has put a mechanism in place that will lead to promotion. That mechanism is: faithfulness.

God Is Faithful

Let's take a moment to look at why God places such a high value on faithfulness. God appreciates faithfulness because faithfulness is part of His nature.

God is not going to back out on you, fail to keep His promises, or disappear. God is our standard, He is not going to change. He is absolutely trustworthy. When it comes to faithfulness, God is our example. Here is proof that God is faithful:

- *"...he is the faithful God..."* (Deuteronomy 7:9).
- *"...he is faithful in all he does"* (Psalm 33:4).
- *"God...is faithful"* (1 Corinthians 1:9).
- *"The one who calls you is faithful..."* (1 Thessalonians 5:24).
- *"...the Lord is faithful..."* (2 Thessalonians 3:3).
- *"...for he who promised is faithful"* (Hebrews 10:23).

God is looking for someone who can be faithful. In the Hebrew language, the word "faithfulness" comes from the same root word as "trust, loyalty, integrity, and steadfastness." God wants us to be just like Him.

The Faithful Hall of Fame

How much does God appreciate faithfulness? Many of the greatest people in the Bible are celebrated, not because of their great accomplishments, but because of their faithfulness.

- Moses was faithful (Numbers 12:7, Hebrews 3:5).
- David was faithful (1 Kings 3:6).
- Hezekiah was faithful (2 Chronicles 31:20).
- Paul was faithful (1 Timothy 1:12).
- Timothy was faithful (1 Corinthians 4:17).
- The saints of Ephesus were faithful (Ephesians 1:1).
- Tychicus was declared faithful twice (Ephesians 6:21; Colossians 4:7).
- The brothers of Colosse were faithful (Colossians 1:2).
- Epaphras was faithful (Colossians 1:7).
- Onesimus was faithful (Colossians 4:9).
- Silas was faithful (1 Peter 5:12).
- Anipas was faithful unto death (Revelation 2:13).

God valued each of these people for their faithfulness. Have you ever heard of Epaphras before? What about Tychicus? The interesting thing about these men is that the Bible does not tell us how many people are in their congregations, or how big their ministries are. Today ministers are often judged by these standards. No, all we know is they are faithful. For God, this is enough. These men continued fighting until the fight was won. Step by step, day by day, they did what was right.

Many begin the race, but few finish. Beginning is easy, but God is looking for those who run the race all the way to the end. Crossing the finish line can only be accomplished through faithfulness.

Faithfulness Guarantees Promotion

When God searches for someone to promote He does not ask, "Has she great natural abilities? Is he thoroughly educated? Is he a fine singer? Is he eloquent in prayer? Can he speak well?" Instead, God asks, "Is he faithful? Is she willing to be used? Are they obedient? Is she willing to serve Me in the little things?"

I saw a plaque on the wall of a church in Jamaica that said, "Great occasions for serving God come seldom. But little ones surround us daily." D. L. Moody explained, "There are many of us who are willing to do great things for the Lord, but few of us are willing to do little things." George Verwer said, "Most Christians want all of the privileges and none of the responsibilities."

Remember, small opportunities are often the beginning of big enterprises. Do your job and then some. There are no traffic jams when you go the extra mile. Any dead fish can float downstream, but it takes a live fish to swim upstream. Remember, the top of the ladder starts at the bottom.

Abraham Lincoln was born in a log house, but he ended his life in the White House. He is famous, not because of where he was born, but because of where he ended up. You never stub your toe standing still, but neither do you go anywhere. Take a chance by taking a step.

Do not despise the day of small beginnings (Zechariah 4:10). The only one who starts at the top is a person digging a ditch. Many things start modestly, but become significant. A single square of old cloth is used as the centerpiece of a beautiful quilt. A grain of sand helps form part of a precious stained-glass window. One dollar invested wisely becomes a fortune. A simple idea scribbled on a dirty napkin grows into a business empire. A humble gatekeeper may one day be entrusted with the temple's treasury.

No one achieves greatness overnight. There is a step-by-step process that brings people to greatness. Do not worry about where you start; be excited about where you will finish. *"...though you started with little, you will end with much"* (Job 8:7 NLT). The NIV reads, *"Your beginnings will seem humble, so prosperous will your future be."*

- 🕮 Moses was a stutterer who became a deliverer.

- 🕮 Gideon was a farmer who became a general.

- 🕮 Deborah was a housewife who became a judge.

- 🕮 David was a shepherd who became a king.

- 🕮 Elisha was a servant who became a prophet.

- 🕮 Esther was an orphan who became a queen.

- 🕮 Peter was a fisherman who became a preacher.

Dream BIG with God

In God's Kingdom there are no little people. Every person is important. Neither are there little jobs. Little jobs lead to big responsibilities. Everything in God's Kingdom starts small and ends BIG.

God is anxiously waiting for you to become as BIG as He already sees you. God sees you BIG even when you think you are small. When the twelve spies explored the promised land, ten of them returned with a bad report. They fearfully announced, "There are giants in the land. We are like grasshoppers in their eyes." The size of the problem they faced made them look small in their own eyes.

But Joshua and Caleb looked at the situation from a God-eyed viewpoint. They told the Israelites, "Do not be afraid of the people of the land, because we will swallow them up. Their protection is gone, but the Lord is with us." These two courageous men put God into the picture. When you put God into the equation of your life, what is small becomes BIG, the difficult becomes easy, and the impossible becomes possible.

All twelve spies saw the same situation, but ten thought the Israelites were grasshopper-sized and two saw themselves God-sized. You may feel small but God does not see you as you are, but as what you could become.

Since every person is BIG in God's eyes, He would never put anyone in a small place. At times we may feel stuck in a small place, but with God there are no little people and no little jobs. Every individual part of the body is important to the whole. The place you are now is vital because it is training you for your destiny. Today's job is preparing you for a future assignment.

In heaven you will be surprised at the vastness of your reward when compared with the smallness of your sacrifice and work. You will receive big rewards for little work.

The power to win must come from within. Take pride in how far you have come; have faith in how far you can go. The difference between extraordinary and ordinary is that little extra.

Be Faithful

- As a volunteer at church, be faithful to complete your assignment.
- As a husband or a wife, be faithful to your spouse.
- As an employee, be faithful to do your job.
- As a parent, be faithful to raise your children to love God.
- As a student, be faithful to complete your homework.
- As a homeowner, be faithful to pay your bills.
- In each role you play in life, strive to be faithful.

Characteristics of a Faithful Person

A faithful person realizes promotion rests in his or her own hands. According to Revelation 17:14, the followers of Jesus have three characteristics. They are: called, chosen, and faithful. Let's look at these three qualifications of a successful believer. Our calling has nothing to do with us. Jeremiah the prophet was called before he was conceived in his mother's womb. Being chosen for a particular task is not in our hands either, it depends upon God's election. But our faithfulness depends solely upon our own choices. One-third of the equation for spiritual success rests in our hands. You are called by God. You have been chosen to accomplish great exploits for heaven. But your level of faithfulness determines the results your life creates. Promotion comes from the Lord, but the one thing we can do to help the process is: Be faithful.

A faithful person moves before he or she is asked. He anticipates needs and fills them before the need is even known. You never have to look to see if a faithful person is there, he or she is just there. My friend Emmanuel is a faithful friend. If I am moving furniture, he immediately brings his pickup truck and helps me load the furniture. If I am out of town and need someone to check my mail, Emmanuel checks the mail. If I need a ride to the airport at six in the morning, guess who is willing to give me a ride? On our international trips, he comes and works hard to take care of our ministry groups. He is a faithful friend who is always there when I need him.

A faithful servant does more than he or she is asked. He uses the G.E.M. principle, he Goes the Extra Mile.

A faithful person is faithful for life. Faithfulness is a lifetime commitment. When I married my wife Jessica, I promised to be faithful to her for the rest of my life. I cannot be 90 percent faithful; I am either faithful or I am not. It is impossible to be faithful "most of the time." My wife would be seriously upset if I was unfaithful to her one day a year. If I argued, "Honey, I am faithful to you the other 364 days of the year," she would have a fit and rightfully so. If I quit or give up on any task God has given me, I will not hear those words, "Well done, My good and faithful servant."

One day of unfaithfulness can destroy years of faithfulness. I know a minister who was very successful and was impacting the world, but one day he made a mistake that destroyed his ministry. In one day the tower he built crumbled. Your potential for blessing people through your faithfulness is directly proportional to your potential for hurting them because of unfaithfulness.

A faithful person stays committed. My commitment to faithfulness is easy. All I have to do is hold on for another sixty or seventy years! I will be judged and tested on what God told me to do. How I use my time, talents, relationships, and resources will be judged by whether I accomplish what He has assigned me to do. Many start the race but few finish. I intend to finish my race; I do not intend to mess up, blow up, burn up, or end up a trash heap beside the road.

But, if I do make a mistake God will not abandon me because even if I am faithless, God is still faithful. When Peter denied Christ, God still loved him and ultimately Peter became one of the greatest leaders in the early Church. We should do everything we can to serve God faithfully, but when our strength runs out, we can rely on God's strength in us.

A faithful person stays faithful in both good times and bad times. It is easy to be faithful when the sun is shining, but a truly faithful person will stick around even when the clouds are gray and the rain is falling. One Sunday I may fly across the country to preach at a church of ten thousand people; another Sunday I drive three-and-a-half hours to preach at a church of twenty people where the offering barely covers the cost of gas. But, I give both services the same energy. Wherever I am, whether I am ministering to a huge crowd or a tiny Bible study, I try to give my all. Why? Because I must continue to be faithful with the small things in order for God to allow me to do big things.

In the beginning of my ministry I would have been overjoyed to be given the opportunity to preach to a crowd of twenty people, now sometimes I ask myself if I am wasting my time ministering to so few. But, I think God still allows me to minister in smaller settings on a regular basis in order to test my heart. No matter how big my ministry gets, I must continue to prove I have the heart of a servant. The masses of people must never be more important than the opportunity to show the love of God to one individual. God's rewards are not based on the size of my ministry on earth, but on the degree of my faithfulness in doing what I am called to do.

A faithful person finds his or her job and does it. God has a specific assignment that you and you alone can do. God has a specific job for you. *"...God has arranged the parts in the body, every one of them, just as he wanted them to be"* (1 Corinthians 12:18). God prepared this job for you before you were even born. *"For we are God's workmanship, created in Christ Jesus to do good works, which God prepared in advance for us to do"* (Ephesians 2:10). If you do not do your job, something important will be left undone. If one part of the body is missing, the body is handicapped. Every person must be in the proper place, or there will be a lack in the Body of Christ.

A faithful person is found doing what he was last told to do. Faithfulness is following the last instruction you received from God. Often God cannot promote you because He is trying to get you to do the last thing He told you to do. Until you pass the same test you have been failing your whole life, God cannot promote you. Everybody wants promotion, but you have to pass the test of faithfulness first. There can be no promotion until faithfulness is proven.

A faithful person uses Satan's attacks to build spiritual muscle. Every attack of Satan is going to attack your faithfulness. The enemy will lie, "You don't have to keep your word." Or "You don't need to show up at church." Or "One little sin will not hurt you." This pressure will try to prevent you from being faithful. We should use Satan's pressure as exercise equipment to build our spiritual muscles. By staying faithful in the midst of temptation, we become spiritually mature.

A faithful person realizes promotion takes time. In our fast food society, we want to be saved on Sunday, filled with the Spirit on Monday, and be Billy Graham on Tuesday. But God takes time to prepare us. Charles Neiman said, "The greatest friend a minister has is time." If you will stay faithful and focused over a period of years, you will be successful. Bob Yandian noted, "We are not in a sprint, we are in a marathon." Christian success is slow-cooked in a Crock-Pot, not a microwave. Faithfulness is not a one-time event; it is a way of life. Faithfulness cannot be proven over the weekend.

Three Things Jesus says to be Faithful Over (Luke 16:10-12):

1. Be faithful over the little.

2. Be faithful over money.

3. Be faithful over that which belongs to another.

Faithfulness Is the Secret to Lasting Success

Secular businesses try to find able people and make them faithful, but God finds faithful people and makes them able. The world does not initially look for faithfulness in a person, rather it looks for ability. But faithfulness is more important. Ability without faithfulness results only in short-term success. Frequently, the initial success of a talented person is short-circuited by a lack of faithfulness.

For example, King Saul was an able leader, but he failed in life because he was not faithful to the commands of God. Saul was *"...an impressive young man without equal among the Israelites—a head taller than any of the others"* (1 Samuel 9:2). He was tall, talented, and had more abilities than anyone else. But when he disobeyed God's direct command, his lack of faithfulness caused the loss of his kingdom. God said, *"I am grieved that I have made Saul king, because he has turned away from me and has not carried out my instructions..."* (1 Samuel 15:11).

Ability determines what you are given. Faithfulness determines what you get to keep. Faithfulness will keep you where talent brings you. People do not remember how fast you get to the top, they remember how long you stay there.

You are like an iceberg. Your abilities are like the 10 percent of an iceberg that sticks above the water, and your character is like the 90 percent of the iceberg below water. Everyone can see your abilities, but your destiny is determined by the part inside you no one can see. Your character is revealed by your faithfulness.

No one becomes a success or failure overnight. Many years of faithfulness contribute to every successful life, and many little failures end in one big failure. Show me someone who is a failure and I will show you how he failed one choice at a time. Show me a successful winner and I will show you how she became a winner by taking small steps towards success on a consistent basis. Where you are today (good or bad) is the result of yesterday's faithfulness or lack thereof.

In life, faithfulness in the small things gets you to your destination. In a trans-oceanic flight from New York to London, a small navigational error of only one degree could send you to Timbuktu instead of England. You must continually check the compass of your life to make sure you are faithful to God's map for your life. If you do, you will experience great rewards!

The Rewards of Faithfulness

1. **Faithfulness attracts God's attention.** *"My eyes will be on the faithful in the land, that they may dwell with me..."* (Psalm 101:6).

2. **Faithfulness releases God's blessings.** *"A faithful man will be richly blessed..."* (Proverbs 28:20).

3. **Faithfulness gives God the opportunity to prove Himself faithful to you.** The Psalmist wrote about God, *"To the faithful you show yourself faithful..."* (Psalm 18:25).

4. **Faithfulness produces safety and security.** *"...The LORD preserves the faithful..."* (Psalm 31:23).

5. **Faithfulness guarantees God's protection.** *"...the LORD...will not forsake his faithful ones. They will be protected forever..."* (Psalm 37:28).

6. **Faithfulness releases reward.** *"The LORD rewards every man for his...faithfulness..."* (1 Samuel 26:23).

7. **Faithfulness in small things leads to big things.** *"...You have been faithful with a few things; I will put you in charge of many things..."* (Matthew 25:21).

8. **Faithfulness protects you from accusations of wrongdoing.** In Daniel 6:4, no fault or wrong could be found in Daniel because he was a faithful servant.

9. **Faithfulness is valuable because of its rarity.** *"Most men will proclaim each his own goodness, but who can find a faithful man?"* (Proverbs 20:6 NKJV).

Obed-Edom started small but ended big. He reaped the rewards of faithfulness. Obed-Edom is a doorkeeper for the ark, but guess what? His story is not finished yet.

CHAPTER 8

THE SECRET
OF
PROMOTION

*"[King David appointed Obed-Edom] to minister
before the ark of the Lord, to make petition,
to give thanks, and to praise the Lord, the God of Israel."*

(1 CHRONICLES 16:4)

A hubbub of activity surrounded the temple one morning when King David arrived for an impromptu visit. All of the people serving in the temple from priests to gatekeepers assembled hurriedly together in the courtyard.

"People from all four corners of the kingdom of Israel have been visiting the temple lately, straining the capacity of every worker. I have decided to create a new position in the temple. Some of the very best among you will be promoted to serve as ministers in the house of God. Your chief responsibilities will be to minister before the ark of the Lord, pray for people as they arrive, give thanks, and you will praise the Lord, the God of Israel."

As King David and his entourage toured the temple, he asked each department supervisor to recommend workers who were doing a good job. Over and over again he heard the name "Obed-Edom."

"Obed-Edom was the best gatekeeper I ever had. I really liked the way he shared his testimony tirelessly," said the head gatekeeper.

"He is an anointed harp player. He worships God with such simplicity and purity of heart," said the worship leader.

"Obed-Edom has been very faithful, especially as a doorkeeper for the ark. I can really see God's hand of blessing on him over these many years," said the high priest.

"Obed-Edom encourages us when we are tired; he never seems to be weary or sick," said the other doorkeepers. "He is a friend to all."

King David was overwhelmed with the positive reports. He was impressed how a man of humble beginnings had such a heart after God. It reminded him of his own long journey from shepherd boy to king of Israel. He chose Obed-Edom as one of the newly appointed ministers.

During the ordination ceremony the following day, the high priest spoke briefly of Obed-Edom. "This man kneeling before you now has been ordained a minister in the house of God. But his ministry did not begin today. He has been ministering ever since he arrived at the temple. As a gatekeeper, he shared his testimony with all who came to visit. He told those who entered what God had done in his life. As a musician Obed-Edom worshiped God with all his heart, and as a doorkeeper he demonstrated his willingness to serve. We are looking for true servants in the house of God and Obed-Edom has proved he has the heart of a servant."

"Praise the Lord!" the servants cheered. The usually quiet demeanor of the doorkeepers suddenly overflowed with joy as they joined in shouting to the glory of God for the promotion of their friend.

Obed-Edom slowly rose to his feet and stood silent, humbled by the speech. He bowed his head and silently prayed, "Lord, help me be able to minister to the people in Your presence. I promise to honor You and do exactly as You ask of me." To that brief but sincere prayer Obed-Edom heard God whisper, "Well done, My good and faithful servant."

Are You Ready to Be Promoted?

Obed-Edom's ministry did not begin the day King David put him in the position of being a minister. I believe his ministry began back when Obed-Edom started as a gatekeeper. I think he stood by the temple gates and ministered to every person who arrived at the temple. As families walked through the gates, he would greet them and begin to tell his testimony. "Did you know the ark was in my house for three months? I was so blessed. Let me tell you how blessed I am!" Obed-Edom would say excitedly.

We tend to make ministry complicated. Some go to seminary for years to learn how to become a minister. But ministry is actually easy. Ministry is simply telling people, "This is what God did for me, and what He did for me, He will do for you." The only legitimate message we can preach is our own story.

Are you in full-time ministry? If you answer "yes" you might be a pastor, an evangelist, or a missionary, but if you answer "no" you would be mistaken. Everyone in the church, regardless of their job, should be a full-time minister. You might be a part-time businessman, housewife, or auto mechanic, but you can be an all-the-time minister.

See yourself as part of the staff of your church. Now, you may not receive a salary. Some staff are paid, some volunteer, and some do such a great job volunteering that they grow into a salary. But, regardless, you should consider yourself as much a part of the ministry of the church as the pastor.

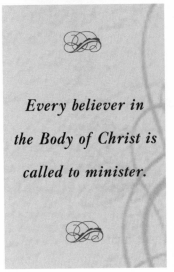

Every believer in the Body of Christ is called to minister.

If God has done a miracle in your life, you are qualified to be a minister. God brings you through tests so you will have a testimony. He pulls you out of a mess, so you will have a message. God delivers you from the fire so you can be on fire for Him.

Every believer in the Body of Christ is called to minister. Nobody is excluded. Everyone is included. The church is more than an organization; it is an organism. We are a Body and every part of the Body has a role.

Buddy Bell says, "God never intended for any believer to be a pew-sitter week after week. He put you in the church to help. Where people do not help, the Body of Christ is weak."

A son complained to his mother, "I don't want to go to church." She replied, "You have to go." "I don't wanna go," the son said again. "Son, you have to go, you're the pastor!" A pastor does not have the option of whether he shows up on Sunday morning or not, neither should any of the other ministers. We have to shift from looking at going to church as an option, to seeing it as an opportunity.

Promotion Comes from Faithfulness

Do you want God to promote you? King David promoted Obed-Edom because of his faithfulness. Let me give you an example from my life about how promotion works.

My parents became missionaries in the country of Mexico when I was ten years old. Since they were my legal guardians, I had to go with them. My ministry started when my father asked me to play the part of

Jesus in a drama for the children's fiestas we did as an outreach for small Mexican churches.

My sister Esther pretended to be a cripple and when Jesus touched her, suddenly she could dance. My other sister Melody pretended to be blind. Jesus spit on the ground, made some mud, but before He could put the mud on her eyes, she was already healed.

Then my father announced, "Now we are going to crucify Jesus." Suddenly, I did not want to play the part of Jesus any longer.

But, my brother Stephen loved his part. Since he was my little brother, I felt it was my prerogative to beat up on him. However, in this drama, he was the Roman soldier, and he got to beat up on Jesus.

He acted with enthusiasm, laughing loudly as he whipped Jesus. To be honest, I think he overacted a little bit.

One day Stephen decided, "This drama is not realistic enough, we need some blood." That day, he brought a big bottle of ketchup and poured it over the whip. The result was like a scene from Mel Gibson's movie, "The Passion of the Christ." Jesus' back was covered in blood.

I told my father, "It is very difficult to hang on the cross. Please preach quickly!" But like most preachers, he did not know how to preach quickly. From Genesis to Revelation, he took his time sharing the gospel story.

As he preached, every fly in Mexico was attracted to the ketchup on my back. With the little insects crawling up and down my body, I prayed, "God, forgive my father for he knows not what he does." Then I hung my head and pretended to die.

One time a kid wanted to know if Jesus was really dead so he started to tickle the bottom of my feet. I suffered for the sake of the cross! Jesus said, "Take up your cross and follow Me." I had many chances to obey Him literally.

When I became a teenager my ministry opportunities expanded. Stephen and I learned how to juggle and ride unicycles. We started doing clown shows at churches all over America. Parents fed their kids donuts and coffee and dropped them off at children's church for us to take care of. For two hours we worked hard to minister to fifty hyperactive kids bouncing off the walls.

Today, God is using me to minister to huge crowds of people in countries around the world. The same messages I used to preach to fifty hyperactive kids, God now gives me the opportunity to preach to crowds that often exceed fifty thousand people in size.

It is amazing how God promotes those who are faithful. Ten years ago, I was preaching to fifty kids, today I am preaching to fifty thousand people. Give me ten more years and I expect to lead one million people to Jesus in a single service!

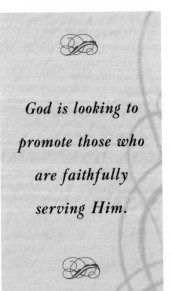

God is looking to promote those who are faithfully serving Him.

Reinhard Bonnke once told me, "That which is considered great today will be normal tomorrow." God is looking to promote those who are faithfully serving Him. As you serve God faithfully, He will expand your ministry opportunities and promote you to a higher level of influence than you ever thought possible.

How Does Promotion Come?

Promotion does not come from man, but from the Lord. God is the One who promotes you for your faithfulness. *"For promotion cometh neither from the east, nor from the west, nor from the south"* (Psalm 75:6 KJV) *"…it is God who judges: He brings one down, he exalts another"* (Psalm 75:7).

God wants to lift you up, expand your influence, and increase your responsibility. Our walk with God is one of continual promotion as we prove ourselves faithful. As the Psalmist said, "[Those who dwell in God's house] *go from strength to strength, till each appears before God…"* (Psalm 84:7).

No one becomes great overnight. David was anointed as a boy to be king, but he did not become king until he was thirty years old. There is always a time gap between the anointing and the appointing.

Before you can be promoted, you must have deep foundations. My office is on the thirty-seventh floor of a sixty-story skyscraper. In the lobby are huge steel-reinforced concrete pillars that extend hundreds of feet underground. It took far more time to sink those pillars down to bedrock, than to build up into the sky. Downward preparation always takes more time than upward progress. The taller the building, the deeper the foundation must be dug.

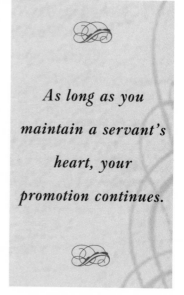

As long as you maintain a servant's heart, your promotion continues.

God will promote you when He knows you are ready to be promoted. Promotion comes because of faithfulness at your present job. Joseph was promoted from the pit to the palace because he was faithful to serve even in the worst of conditions. You will never be promoted until you have mastered the job you are currently doing. Promotion is a reward for doing your current job with excellence. You will never be promoted for doing a job poorly.

Promotion never comes when we think we deserve it, but when God thinks we deserve it.

The Lord determines how high you will be promoted. As long as you maintain a servant's heart, your promotion continues. As soon as you lose the heart of a servant, your demotion begins. What God promotes He can demote. God lifts up kings and puts down kings. He lifts the humble and puts down the proud.

Promotions often come disguised as more work. The higher you are in the Kingdom, the more people you are called to serve. Robb Thompson says, "Promotion is never granted for performing the tasks you are already paid to do, promotion comes by doing more than is expected of you."

My Discovery About Destiny

One year after the devastating terrorist attacks on September 11, 2001, my entire family visited New York City for some sightseeing. The first thing we wanted to view was the memorial for the victims, so we looked for a parking spot near Ground Zero. Finding parking in downtown New York was like trying to find a needle in a haystack. My mother finally dropped the rest of the family off and continued to search for parking.

We walked around Ground Zero, toured a nearby eighteenth-century church, and viewed pictures of victims lost in the tragedy. My mother called; she had finally found a place to park! Once the family was reunited, we decided to visit the Empire State Building.

After the Twin Towers fell, the Empire State Building reclaimed its title as the tallest building in New York City's skyline. We could see the spire of it peeking out from behind other buildings. Since it appeared to be about ten blocks away, we decided to walk to the Empire State Building.

As my family strolled down Broadway on this sunny afternoon, the numerous shops, the busy traffic, and the strange variety of people astonished us. After walking ten blocks, the Empire State Building did not appear any closer than when we had started. We continued walking. Soon, we had walked over twenty city blocks. We were in the middle of a park and had completely lost sight of the building.

We debated whether we should turn back and get our car or whether we should keep walking. We decided to keep walking. Surely it was close! After another hour of trekking through traffic, we wearily arrived at the Empire State Building. We were exhausted, out of breath, footsore and thirsty, but after ascending the tower in a series of elevators, we celebrated because we had made it!

The view was breathtakingly beautiful. We could see the Statue of Liberty, Times Square, Central Park, and hundreds of skyscrapers of varying heights. Way off in the distance we could barely see Ground Zero where we had begun our journey. In order to avoid finding a new parking space, my family had walked over thirty-two city blocks!

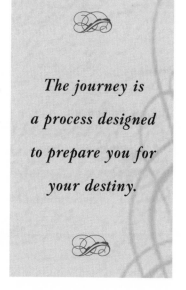

The journey is a process designed to prepare you for your destiny.

Every step of the journey was worth it. Believe me, if we had known the building was farther than ten blocks, we would not have attempted to walk. But since we did, that day will be remembered as one of the best days of our lives. Not only did we get the scenic tour of New York City, we also had a wonderful time as a family.

Later I realized our journey that day could be compared to what many of us go through as we travel the path of becoming what God has called us to become.

Here are some of the truths I learned:

1. **Because your destiny is so big, it may appear to be closer than it really is.** In the beginning of our journey, the Empire State Building seemed near. Later we discovered the reason it looked deceptively close was because it was so much bigger than all the buildings surrounding it. Right now, your destiny may appear to be really close. Do not be surprised if it takes longer to arrive than expected. God's final destiny for your life is so big, it is probably farther off in the distance than you think. Meanwhile, do not be discouraged. The journey is a process designed to prepare you for your destiny.

2. **There are many tempting distractions on the way to your destiny.** New York City is full of interesting sights and entertaining places. We passed thirty-two blocks of distractions but stayed focused on our goal by continuing to walk in a straight line. Do not get distracted by street-level views while on your journey to a higher level.

3. **In the middle of your journey, you may lose sight of your destination.** Halfway through our journey we lost sight of the Empire State Building. We were forced to ask for directions to make sure we were still on the right path. In the journey of life, never be afraid to ask for directions if you lose sight of your destiny. Seek God's guidance. Your steps are ordered by the Lord. Ask advice from a godly mentor who has been where you want to go.

4. **If you settle for "average" you will never arrive at "great."** On our walk to the tallest building in New York City we passed hundreds of other tall buildings. In any other city in the world, each of those buildings would have been impressive. We could have been satisfied with seeing one of the shorter buildings, but instead we

continued to seek for the best. In your search for the destiny God has called you to, do not be satisfied with mediocrity. You may relinquish many good things in order to achieve great things.

5. **Never give up!** I was tired, my feet were sore, and I was thirsty, but I continued to trudge along. The journey of a thousand miles is taken one step at a time. No matter how you feel, keep walking and eventually you will reach your God-given destiny.

6. **Someone will try to discourage you.** We asked one man for directions and he laughed at us. He said we would never reach the Empire State Building. Then he asked, "Why do you want to go there anyway?" Finally, he predicted it would rain before we would arrive and the elevators would be shut down. When people speak words of doubt about your destiny, ignore them. Surround yourself with people who believe in you and your destiny.

7. **Your destiny will be worth every step of the journey.** My family spent over two hours on top of the Empire State Building because we were having so much fun. My parents kissed as the sun set over the famous city skyline. We watched as thousands of lights flickered to life as far as the eye could see. It was an experience we will never forget. It was worth the trouble it took for our family to arrive there. During the journey you might question the value of achieving God's destiny for your life, but once you arrive you will realize that every step was worthwhile.

Once you arrive you will realize that every step was worthwhile.

8. **Keep your eyes on the sky or you will miss your destination.** When we finally arrived at the Empire State Building we

almost passed it because our eyes were looking downward. The bottom of the building looks the same as every other building, but once we looked upwards, we realized we had arrived. If you look down, all you see is defeat (de feet), but if you look up, you will see your destiny.

So, now Obed-Edom has been promoted to be a minister, but guess what? His story is not finished yet.

CHAPTER 9

LEADERSHIP IN THE HOUSE OF GOD

"[King David] left Obed–Edom and his sixty-eight associates to minister with them...."

(1 CHRONICLES 16:38)

Obed-Edom peered sharply at the sixty-eight men surrounding him ready to follow his leadership. His group was responsible for guarding the east gate and for protecting the temple storehouses. Their daily devotional was about to begin.

"Friends, have you ever wondered what God has in store for you?" Obed-Edom asked in an authoritative but gentle voice. "Your eyes have not seen, your ears have not heard, neither has your heart imagined the great plans God has for your life. Just look at what God has done in my life. I was nobody. I did not have any relatives in the royal court or a rich father-in-law to promote me. Now I am a leader in the house of God."

One curious man raised his hand, "How did you become such a great leader?"

"God came to live in my house," Obed-Edom explained. "The secret to my success is simple. His presence changed my life forever. When I was young I never dreamed I would be where I am today. I just had a burning desire to be close to God's presence. When I came to the house of God, I was willing to serve in any way I could. If they had asked me to sweep the temple steps, I would have been happy to help."

"How can we become a leader like you?" a young novice asked eagerly.

"Find a place to serve and then serve with all your heart. The further you go in ministry, the greater your place of service will be. The greatest servant in our land is King David who serves us."

"I thought King David is our ruler," stated another young man.

"Yes, he is a great ruler, but the greatest leaders are those who are the greatest servants. When I started working in God's house, I gave my time, energy, and creativity as a gift to God. As I proved myself faithful, God promoted me to the place where I am today."

"Will God do the same for me?" questioned Shemaiah. This first week as a temple volunteer was a dream come true for Obed-Edom's firstborn son.

"Absolutely! Anyone who serves faithfully in God's house will be promoted by God," Obed-Edom declared. "Now let's get to work."

As Obed-Edom's team marched away to their posts, he called after them, "Remember, serve God with excellence today!"

Shemaiah watched his father with pride and respect as he disappeared across the courtyard and thought, *God has blessed my father with wisdom. I hope to serve God with the same heart he has.* He prayed, "Lord, be my God just as You are for my father. I want to get close to You just like my father did, and I hope to be the best doorkeeper You have ever had. Thank You for letting me see Your glory when I was a little boy. Thank You for coming to my house."

Are You Ready to Be a Leader?

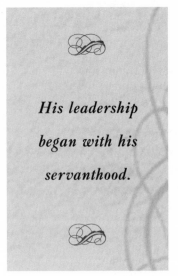

His leadership began with his servanthood.

Now Obed-Edom is a leader with sixty-eight associates to mentor. But his leadership began with his servanthood. As he served God, he attracted like-minded men who followed his example.

God is calling you to be a leader too. You have the potential to lead those in your sphere of influence. But it all begins with your willingness to be a servant.

God wants to promote you from glory to glory. But God works progressively. As you prove yourself faithful at one level, God allows you to go to the next level. However, you cannot skip glories. You don't instantly go from little glory to big glory, from A to Z.

Notice the sequence of Obed-Edom's promotion: gatekeeper, harp player, doorkeeper, minister, leader. As he proved himself faithful in one position, he was promoted to other positions of greater responsibility.

There is no such thing as an overnight success. As one preacher who became famous after twenty years of ministry said, "If I'm an overnight success, it was one long, long night." Every mega-minister has a story about starting out small. Recently I heard Joyce Meyer share at a conference about her beginning. In the early days of her ministry she once traveled hundreds of miles in an old beat-up van to minister to sixty ladies. On the journey home she did not have enough money to afford a hotel room so she slept in her van in the parking lot of a fast food restaurant. Today she touches millions of lives every day. Because of her willingness to serve even in tough conditions, God has made her a leader of leaders.

If King David had asked for temple toilet cleaners that fateful day when Obed-Edom became a doorkeeper, I think Obed-Edom would have eagerly volunteered. Why? Because he was willing to do whatever it took to stay close to the presence of God. We need more people with this attitude in the church today. If you cannot clean up a mess in the bathroom, how can you ever clean up a mess in the pulpit?

Do you want to be a leader? Find a place to serve. The greatest words we will hear in heaven will be, *"Well done, good and faithful servant..."* (Matthew 25:21).

The true path to leadership is through serving others. Jesus said, *"The greatest among you shall be your servant"* (Matthew 23:11). Jesus demonstrated this principle in His own life. He said, *"[I did] not come to be served, but to serve..."* (Mark 10:45). Jesus *"made himself nothing, taking the very nature of a servant..."* (Philippians 2:7). The foundation of Christian life is service. We imitate Christ who gave His life on our behalf. Christ gave His life; we are privileged to do the same.

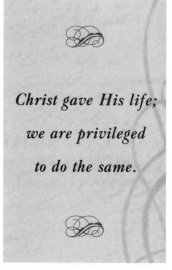

Christ gave His life; we are privileged to do the same.

One example of Christ's radical servant-leadership occurred during the Last Supper. The disciples were arguing about who was the greatest among them, but Jesus proved He was the greatest by silently picking up a basin of water and a towel to wash their dusty feet. He who was Lord of the universe, the One before whom the angels prostrate themselves, the King before whom every knee will eventually bow, knelt down to wash the feet of those who called Him Lord.

The secret to being great, to being at the top, to being the best of the best, is to be a servant. James and John asked to sit at the right hand of Jesus in heaven. They were looking for promotion, but Jesus told them, *"...whoever wants to become great among you must be your servant, and whoever wants to be first must be slave of all"* (Mark 10:43-44). They wanted to be elevated to a position of privilege, but Jesus pointed them toward servanthood.

The only way to serve God here on this earth is by serving people. If you love God, you will love people. If you truly want to serve God, you will serve people.

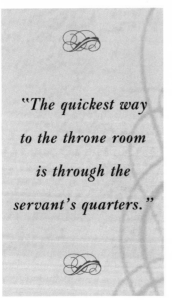

"The quickest way to the throne room is through the servant's quarters."

Servanthood is the path to promotion in the Kingdom of God. John Mason says, "The quickest way to the throne room is through the servant's quarters." Why was the world impressed with Mother Teresa? Was it because of her great clothing, winning smile, wealthy background, or superior education? No. It was because she served those whom no one else would serve. She washed the sores of lepers, nursed the HIV victims, clothed the orphans, and fed the street beggars of Calcutta, India. People credited her with being a saint because she was willing to be a servant. Mother Teresa once said, "We can do no great things, only small things with great love."

Calling someone a "servant-leader" does not make sense at first. The term is an oxymoron. How can I be both a servant and a leader? But, it can be understood when you realize that the world's system and God's system work exactly opposite. If you want to live, Jesus said you must die. If you want to receive, you must give. If you want to be the greatest, you must become the least. If you want to rule, you must serve.

Servanthood Leads to Promotion.

Do you think you deserve a promotion? The equation is simple: If you don't serve, you don't deserve! Hidden within every position of servanthood is an opportunity for promotion.

True servants become true leaders. Leaders are simply servants who serve more people. The more you are promoted, the greater your level of service. Genuine leadership is servant-leadership. Until you learn to serve, you will never become a leader.

Your attitude as a servant determines the timing of your promotion. If you do not serve well, you will never be more than a servant. But if you serve faithfully, the day will come when you will be much more than a servant.

Being a servant makes you humble. Being humble makes you great. Jesus said, *"For whoever exalts himself will be humbled, and whoever humbles himself will be exalted"* (Matthew 23:12). That is why Scripture says: *"God opposes the proud but gives grace to the humble"* (James 4:6). If you think you are qualified you probably are not ready to be promoted.

The Greek word which is translated as "servant" is *doulos* which actually means "slave" or "bondman" or "one under another's authority." Paul repeatedly used this word to refer to himself as a "servant (or slave) of Jesus Christ." Even though Paul was in a position of leadership in the early Church, he recognized that his primary calling was to be a servant.

God never promotes us until we are overqualified for the position we are in. Many times I have overestimated my own abilities, anointing, and level of maturity. I used to sit in the back row of a minister's conference and mumble to myself, "I am a better minister then the person speaking. I have more revelation and talent. Why don't they ask me to speak?" I failed to realize I was not ready for the opportunity. I had more growing up and maturing to do. I needed more wisdom, more experience. I had to learn how to serve better in the position where I was before I was qualified to lead. It was ten years from the time I thought I was qualified to minister at that conference to the time I was invited to speak at that same conference.

If you have not been promoted, it may be because you have not completely learned how to serve at the level you are at. Your willingness to complete a distasteful task qualifies you to be promoted.

There is a huge difference in attitude between an employee and a true servant. Employees are paid by man, but servants are rewarded by God. An employee looks for what he can get from working, a servant looks for what he can give by working. Some have the attitude, "I'm just working because I have to." Others realize they are only playing the part of a servant until they prove themselves worthy of a better position.

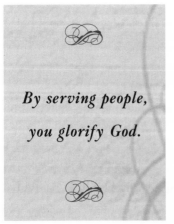

By serving people, you glorify God.

Many say they want to serve Christ, but few want to serve His Bride. If Jesus walked into your house, how would you treat Him? Would you offer Him a cold drink? Cook Him a gourmet meal? Wash His feet? Give Him a ride in your car? Imagine if your pastor visited your house. How would you serve him or her? Imagine a homeless man knocks on the door. How would you react?

Gandhi, the father of modern India, said, "Service of man is worship of God." By serving people, you glorify God. Jesus originated this idea when He said, *"...whatever you did for one of the least of these brothers of mine, you did for me"* (Matthew 25:40). Even when serving people, we are really serving God. No matter who you serve here on earth, you should always *"Serve wholeheartedly, as if you were serving the Lord, not men"* (Ephesians 6:7).

A Place for Every Servant

Having the attitude of a servant will never go out of style. One sure guarantee of success is to maintain a servant's demeanor. Servants get noticed and promoted. There will always be a job for the true servant.

Our natural human tendency is to expect others to serve us. We demand our rights and list the reasons why we deserve to be served. At restaurants we complain if our water glass is not filled promptly. But we should be like Jesus and look for ways to serve people instead of demanding that others serve us.

Life is like tennis; the better you serve, the more points you win. In every area of life, there is an opportunity to serve. Marriage is about serving your spouse. Your job is about serving your boss. Church is about serving God and people. Parents serve their children and children should serve their parents. Businesses must serve the needs of their customers if they expect to stay in business. Even fast food restaurants are looking for people who can serve with a friendly smile.

A Servant for Every Place

Pastors and church leaders, I want to take a moment to encourage you. It may feel like you are the only sacrificial servant in your church, but God has called someone to fill every need in your church. It is time to give believers the opportunity to serve. We must train and release people into ministry positions. Every believer is called to be a minister.

Remember the advice of Jethro, Moses' father-in-law, when Moses was overworked and overwhelmed? He told Moses to appoint leaders and divide responsibility for all the work. We should do the same in our churches.

Armor Bearer, Not Gummy Bear

In ancient Israel during times of war an armor bearer was assigned to follow the king and help carry his weapons. Today there are people who are called to be armor bearers to their pastors by helping with the work of the ministry. Unfortunately, many armor bearers act more like gummy bears. They appear sweet, but when there is work to be done they lack backbone.

Sometimes I get a laugh out of watching armor bearers help me. I arrive at a church and suddenly I am surrounded by bodyguards and a large entourage to help carry my Bible and briefcase. What are they protecting me from? And where were these bodyguards when I was preaching in Africa and kids were throwing stones at me? I can make it around the world pulling my suitcase myself and now I need all these people to help me the last twenty feet with my briefcase? But one day I realized the purpose of these armor bearers was not to benefit me, but to benefit them. By helping me, they are preparing for their own promotion.

Faithfulness to Serve God's House

While I was studying theology in college I met some students who criticized various ministries. They used their intellectual prowess to figure out how to run churches better than anyone else. I remember one person saying, "If you give me enough money and people to work for me, I can pastor a bigger church than Joel Osteen and conduct bigger crusades than Billy Graham." I asked him if he was involved in the university's community outreach program that distributed groceries to poor people. He replied, "Oh, I don't do any small ministry. I'm called to do BIG ministry." Do you think he is successful today?

This type of pretentious know-it-all will never accomplish anything for God. Why? God only promotes those who are willing to serve.

When people sit in the pews and never serve, they become spiritually constipated. They are like the Dead Sea. Water comes in, and nothing flows out. The salt builds up and the fish die. The Dead Sea is always receiving, never giving. People like this are good at nothing but complaining.

There will never be a shortage of critics and complainers. Some sit in the pews for years complaining about their church. "The music is too loud. We sang this song last week. The sermons are too long. The pastor's tie is too bright. The carpet is the wrong color." The most infamous complaint of all before they leave the church for good is, "This church does not feed me anymore."

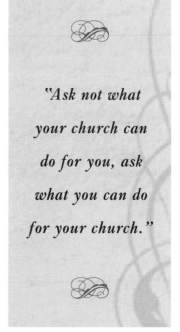

"Ask not what your church can do for you, ask what you can do for your church."

Church hoppers often complain, "This church is just not meeting my needs, I'm finding a new church." Instead of trying to meet the needs of the church, they go looking for a church that can meet their needs. Many become disillusioned and disappointed and some even stop attending church altogether.

Recently I preached at a church where an elderly woman received a reward for maintaining perfect Sunday school attendance for forty years. In all those years she never missed a Sunday. She was faithful. In contrast, some believers switch churches every month. They move around looking for a perfect church, but if they ever joined a perfect church, it would no longer be perfect.

When you hold a seed in your hand it is hard to tell what kind of seed it is, but once it is planted it begins to grow, produces fruit, and its destiny is revealed. Get planted in a local church and be faithful serving where you are planted. If you are having difficulty finding your destiny, it is because you are not planted. Once you are planted, stay faithful. Putting roots down is significant. Trees do not just get up and walk away.

People say, "I want to find a church that can serve me and my needs." WRONG. You need a church that you can serve and fill others' needs. Service builds your spiritual muscles and prepares you to be a champion in God's Kingdom. Your needs will never be met until you help meet the needs of others. Be like Jesus; don't look to be served, look to serve. To paraphrase John F. Kennedy, "Ask not what your church can do for you, ask what you can do for your church."

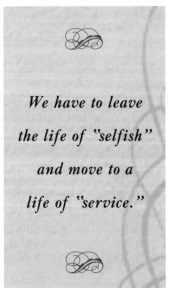

We have to leave the life of "selfish" and move to a life of "service."

The world often asks, "What's in it for me?" As Christians we should ask, "What can I do for you?" We should die to self (self-desires, self-needs, self-ambitions) and live for others. Instead of looking for quality of service, look for opportunities for service. We have to leave the life of "selfish" and move to a life of "service." Stop asking God what He can do for you, and start asking Him how you can be a part of what He is doing.

We go to church, sing a few songs, listen to the preacher for thirty minutes and call it a "service," but true service begins when you walk out the doors of the church. Service is when you "serve" another person. A church service simply prepares us for real acts of service. Church is not supposed to be a spectator sport.

The solution is to get involved. Help solve some of the problems. Ask your pastor what you can do to help. Find someone you can pray with or minister to. When a Native American asked Tommy Barnett why his church in Arizona did not have a ministry to Native Americans, Pastor Tommy looked the man in the eyes and said, "It's because you have not started that ministry yet." He commissioned the man that day to start an outreach to their Native American community. Pastor Barnett believes "the miracle is in the house" meaning that whatever the church needs is already hidden within those who already attend the church.

Serving in the church is God's apprenticeship program. When you prove yourself faithful and obedient in one job, God will promote you to another. If you do not know where to serve, find a need and fill it.

Some people worry about what they are called to do; however, Obed-Edom never received a specific call from God, he simply served. The need was the call. The need is the catalyst for our calling. When you see a problem and say, "Somebody ought to do something," realize that you are the somebody that should do something.

There are no excuses for not serving. I asked one of my friends when he would go on a mission trip. He replied, "I'm waiting for God." I told him, "No! God is waiting for you." Many pray for God to move, but God is often waiting for you to move.

One reward for serving is the potential for enormous personal growth. There are gifts and talents lying dormant inside of you that you do not even know exist. When you find a place to serve, those gifts will be revealed.

What Should Church Look Like?

While looking at a church's website, I found a great description of what church used to look like and what it should look like.

The Old Paradigm of Church

- The church is like a **bank,** providing services to people.

- The pastor and staff **do** all the ministry.

- People attend service and then **go home.**

- Everyone serves God based on how they **feel.**

- The congregation gives **sporadically** to the work of God.

- People are **cold** and **distant** towards one another and **uninvolved** in the lives of fellow church members.

- People live day-to-day lives of **mediocrity,** uninspired to do anything for God.

- People **rarely** share their faith with the lost.

The Obed-Edom Paradigm of Church

- The church is full of people called to **minister.**

- The role of the pastor and staff is to **train** and **equip** people for service.

- People come to church looking for a way to **meet** the needs of others.

- Everyone serves God out of **thankfulness** for His love.

- The congregation gives **enthusiastically** to support the vision of the church.

- People are **warm** and **loving** and develop **close relationships** with others.

- People live **on fire** and **inspired** to accomplish big things for God.

- The church is full of **soulwinners,** who regularly reach out to the lost.

Lessons from the Life of Elijah

A great example of how God promotes servants is found in the story of Elisha. He was a wealthy farmer plowing with twelve pair of oxen when the prophet Elijah called him into ministry. Elisha said good-bye to his parents and then slaughtered his cattle as a sacrifice to God (1 Kings 19:19-21). He gave up everything, even his livelihood, in order to serve Elijah.

At first it looked as if Elisha, by becoming a servant, suffered a demotion. He went from being an independent farmer to being little better than a slave. He went from being the man in charge to following orders. He followed Elijah around and took care of his needs. He polished his sandals, washed his clothes, carried his sermon notes, and scheduled his appointments.

We know now that Elisha was destined to take Elijah's place, but Elisha did not know that. All he knew was that God called him to serve. He was hot, tired, dusty, and sweaty. But, he stuck to his promise to follow Elijah.

His reward came when Elijah was taken up into heaven by God. In payment for his years of service, Elisha received a double dose of his master's anointing and became the new prophet. He went on to do twice as many miracles as his master had done. Because he served faithfully, he was promoted by God to a position of influence.

Elijah had raised up a school of prophets. This group of over fifty ministers watched him preach, sat in his classes, and took notes as Elijah performed miracles. Each of them would have loved to have become Elijah's successor, but none of them were promoted to the coveted position. Only Elisha the servant was promoted. Many wanted Elijah's anointing, many claimed to serve, but only Elisha was a true servant.

Elisha learned that servanthood was the secret to Elijah's success. When Elijah called down fire from heaven he prayed, "Lord...let it be known...that I am thy servant." Why didn't he pray, "Let it be known that I am a prophet, the mighty man of God?" Elijah understood that God is not impressed with titles, but with servanthood. Elisha learned this valuable lesson during his apprenticeship.

Lessons from the Life of Gehazi

Elisha was a servant who became a prophet, but there is another servant who became a leper. His name is Gehazi and he was Elisha's servant. Unfortunately, Gehazi made a terrible mistake that prevented him from being promoted.

When Naaman, an enemy commander, came to be healed by Elisha, it was the perfect opportunity for God to be glorified in the eyes of a heathen (2 Kings 5). Naaman, by following Elisha's instructions, was miraculously healed from leprosy. He offered money as payment for the miracle, but Elisha turned it down because he wanted Naaman to know that miracles cannot be bought.

Gehazi was greedy. He followed Naaman's chariot and lied to him saying Elisha had sent him at the last moment to ask for some money and two sets of clothing. It was a bad idea to try to fool the prophet. Elisha confronted Gehazi and told him that because of his greed, he would be cursed with the same leprosy Naaman had been healed from.

I always wondered why Elisha punished Gehazi so severely. But one day I realized that Elisha did not just consider Gehazi to be a servant, Elisha was grooming him to be the next prophet of Israel. Evidence for this is in the story of the Shunammite woman's son who was brought back to life (2 Kings 4). In this story, Elisha is clearly training Gehazi how to be a prophet. A servant is far more than a servant, a servant is a leader in training.

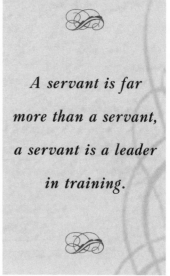

A servant is far more than a servant, a servant is a leader in training.

Gehazi could have experienced twice the anointing of Elisha (four times the anointing of Elijah), but for the sake of a fine set of clothes and a little money, Gehazi threw the opportunity away. He could have been the greatest prophet in the history of Israel. If he had been a true servant he would have seen a day of promotion.

Elisha was disappointed with Gehazi because in his time of servant-hood he learned how to be a good servant. Elisha was upset because he knew what a servant could become. He knew a servant could become a great leader.

My Lesson in Servanthood

Several years ago I traveled to Africa to meet a famous crusade evangelist. This powerful man of God has done massive evangelistic campaigns for over thirty years in countries around the globe and I wanted to learn all I could. I had never met him before and was anxious to make a good first impression. I carefully laid out my best suit, ironed my clean shirt, and picked out a bright tie.

The day he arrived was extremely stressful. The crusade team faced many difficulties. The sound system was three days late arriving because it was delayed passing through borders in an area where civil war was still waging. The truck was even shot at in one rural area. We only had a few hours to assemble the stage and sound system instead of the two days it normally required.

I saw a need and decided to help fill that need. I jumped on the back of the truck and started pulling out pieces of staging along with a local crew. The crusade ground was covered in choking lava dust. I quickly became covered from head to toe with a layer of black soot as I worked to build the stage and sound towers. After several hours of intense labor, I heard one of the team say, "The evangelist is on his way here."

"Oh, no! What is he going to think of me?" I wondered in dismay, "I came all the way to Africa to meet him and now I am covered in dirt. My plans to impress him are destroyed."

The evangelist spied me from the window of his car, streaks of dirt across my face and blackened clothes. He said to himself, "I like this guy already!" Why? Because it was obvious that I was serving.

Our service to God flows from our thankfulness for His blessings.

That night over dinner he invited me to preach at his church, one of the fastest-growing churches in Canada. If I had been dressed up in my nice proper suit, he might have thought I was just another young wannabe preacher. But because I was willing to get my hands dirty, he was impressed from the start.

Wherever you are, be all there. Whatever your hands find to do, do with all your might. Our service to God flows from our thankfulness for His blessings. We are not obligated to serve. We do not have to serve, we get to serve. Look for a way to serve with all your heart and God will promote you to a position of leadership.

Obed-Edom is a leader in the house of God, but guess what? His story is not finished yet.

CHAPTER 10

REVERSE THE CURSE OVER YOUR FAMILY

"Obed-Edom…had sons…. His son Shemaiah
also had sons, who were leaders in their father's
family because they were very capable men."

(1 CHRONICLES 26:4,6)

"My dearest wife, you are the most beautiful grandmother I have ever seen, "Obed-Edom whispered as he snuggled close to his helpmate of over sixty years. "I don't care what anyone says, you don't look a day over fifty."

"I know you're stretching the truth, but I still like what you're saying," his wife whispered back as she kissed his wrinkled forehead tenderly. "The ceremony was so beautiful today as we dedicated our grandson in the temple. He has such a meaningful name, Semakiah. 'Jehovah has sustained.'"

"My name is so horrible," said Obed-Edom sadly, "it means 'slave, enemy of Israel.' My parents did not serve God."

"But you managed to turn the destiny of our family around, my love," encouraged his wife. "Look, I made a list of the meanings of the names of some of our kids and grandkids."

Obed-Edom peered at the scroll his wife handed him.

Our Children

> Shemaiah—Heard by Jehovah
>
> Jehozabad—Jehovah has endowed
>
> Joah—Jehovah is brother
>
> Sacar—Wages
>
> Nethaneel—Given of God
>
> Ammiel—My kinsman is God

Issachar—There is recompense

Peulthai—Work

Our Grandchildren

Othni—Lion of Jehovah

Rephael—Healed of God

Obed—Servant or one who serves

Elzabad—God has given

Elihu—He is my God

Semakiah—Jehovah has sustained

With pride, Obed-Edom remembered the day years ago when his firstborn came to him with an announcement. "Father, I feel God has called me to work with you in the temple."

"Why do you want to follow in my footsteps, Shem?"

"Dad, I've really thought about what I want to do with my life. I want to serve God the way you taught me. I want God to bless me the same way He has blessed you."

"Son, you make me proud. So many kids rebel against their parents and run away from home. I'm thrilled you want to serve God," beamed Obed-Edom.

Obed-Edom turned to his wife, "We are truly blessed, dearest. All of our kids and grandkids are serving God."

"Yes," she replied as she gently lifted his calloused hand into hers, "and I am more blessed than all because I am the wife of the man God chose to bless. Husband, you are loved by God, your children, and the wife of your youth." They drifted contentedly to sleep, hand in hand under the covers.

Raising Champion Children for God

The miracle of Obed-Edom extended beyond his own life. All his children and grandchildren served God in the temple alongside him. Obed-Edom came from a bad family background. He was a slave, an enemy of Israel, and from a lowly city, but because God's presence came to live in his house, he reversed the family curse. He refused to allow his past to determine the future of his family.

You may have come from a shady background, but you can change the destiny of your descendants. Your children do not need to go through the same junk you went through. Your example can set in motion enormous blessing for your entire family.

In the aftermath of a hurricane, a reporter interviewed one of the survivors who said, "My house is under water, everything I own is gone, but I'm just happy my whole family is safe." When disaster hit, he discovered what was most important. Possessions can be replaced. Sentimental heirlooms will be forgotten. Treasures will come and go, but family is forever. How important is your family to you?

Treasures will come and go, but family is forever.

Mothers and fathers express a universal desire for their children to have better education and higher paying jobs than they did, and most importantly of all, to be closer to God then they were. Do you want your children to live a better life then you are living?

When you serve God, the blessing goes far beyond your own life and extends into the lives of your children and grandchildren. You are an example to your children. If they see you are serious about serving God, they will know your relationship with God is real. Do you want your children to serve God?

Children need to see their parents involved at church. If you tell your children to go to church, but do not attend yourself, it will be no surprise when they rebel and run away from God as teenagers. Kids do what you do, not what you say. More is "caught than taught." Like produces like. A redheaded mama and a redheaded daddy will produce redheaded kids. If you want your children to serve God, you need to set a good example by serving in the house of God yourself.

Part of the responsibility of being a parent is to teach your children. The Bible says, *"...He commanded our forefathers to teach their children, so the next generation would know them, even the children yet to be born, and they in turn would tell their children"* (Psalm 78:5-6). God's view extends much further than we can imagine.

Investing in the lives of your children is an investment in eternity. We are in a relay race. God wants us to pass truth to the next generation. We must be diligent not to drop the baton. The truth God has taught you is not meant to die with you. *"Tell it to your children, and let your children tell it to their children, and their children to the next generation"* (Joel 1:3).

I remember walking into children's church as a six-year-old and being greeted by my children's pastor. His name was John Tasch. He planted an amazing amount of vision into my spirit at a tender age. He was totally dedicated to his calling and it showed in all he did. The fruit of his ministry continues in my life and in the lives of hundreds of other children who are now grown up. He daily asked himself this question,

"Where can I best invest my life over the next twenty years to have the greatest effect on the Kingdom of heaven?" His answer? Children!

Children are a blessing from God. Often when we think of blessing, we immediately think of material things. But the Jewish idea of blessing included children. In fact, according to one Jewish tradition, Obed-Edom's wife became pregnant while the ark was in their home and bore all eight sons at one time. I do not know if she really gave birth to octuplets, but regardless, her eight sons were a blessing.

A Great Woman Behind
Every Great Man

Obed-Edom is not the only hero of this story. Mrs. Obed-Edom was just as responsible for all the children serving God. She had eight sons and trained them to follow in her husband's godly footsteps. She was a super Mom.

They say that behind every great man stands a great woman. My mother is one of those great women. She is addicted to the presence of God and has passed her passion on to each of her five children. She demonstrated her fervency for the Lord during two special times each day; morning prayers and evening Bible story time. Every morning before school, my mother scheduled a time for the family to worship God. For ten minutes we sang songs of praise and worship. Then, we prayed together. Finally, we spent ten minutes listening to a preaching tape. Every evening before bedtime my mother read us a Bible story.

My mother is so consumed with the reality of God's presence that she continues the practice to this day. Last time I visited home with my wife, she asked us to sit down and listen to her read a Bible story. I complained, "Mom, I am a grown man. Do I still have to do what I did when I was a

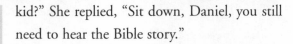

"The only earthy possessions you can take to heaven with you are your children."

kid?" She replied, "Sit down, Daniel, you still need to hear the Bible story."

My mother is a significant source of inspiration in my life. She spent many long hours teaching me the ways of the Lord. She believes, "The only earthy possessions you can take to heaven with you are your children." She made her family her top priority. She made me what I am today.

Begin Training Your Children Now

"Train a child in the way he should go, and when he is old he will not turn from it" (Proverbs 22:6). Imagine a large tree branch. The branch represents an adult. It is set in its ways and it will not bend. It would require a miracle to change the shape of a twisted branch. An adult's life can be changed, but often it takes a miracle from God and a lot of hard work to straighten out a twisted life. Now, imagine a soft, pliable twig. This twig represents a child. It is flexible and easily bent. A child can be easily trained to follow God. When a young sapling is planted, it is often tied to a stake to ensure it grows straight. If you will tie your child close to God's Word, your child will grow strong in faith.

The Great Commission for Parents

Jesus said, *"Let the little children come to me, and do not hinder them, for the kingdom of God belongs to such as these"* (Mark 10:14). It is better to prepare than to repair. It is better to invest time training your children to follow God now than it is to wait until they are grown up to train them.

Any evangelism after high school is not evangelism, but salvage. If you wait until a child is older before you reach him, you have wasted the best training years of his life. It is better to go fishing with your son today than it is to go fishing for him tomorrow.

Have you ever caught a fish over four feet long? Most people have not. But have you ever caught a fish that is only two or three inches long? Many people have. The small fish are easier to catch, but we throw them back into the water so that they will get bigger. But, there is no guarantee that we will catch that fish once it gets bigger. Let's not throw our children back into the water!

Children Have Great Potential

A famous evangelist named D. L. Moody once made a commitment to God. He told God that he would lead someone to Christ every day of his life. One time a friend who knew about this commitment, asked D. L. Moody if anyone had been saved that day.

Mr. Moody responded, "Yes, two-and-a-half people were saved today."

The man was confused. He thought about it and then he asked, "Do you mean two adults and one child were saved?"

D. L. Moody said, "No! Two children and one adult were saved today."

This great evangelist understood that once you reach an adult, half of his life had been wasted. But, if you reach a child, they have their entire life ahead of them to serve God.

We must make time for the children. The Bible reports that when the disciples tried to tell children to go away, because Jesus was too busy, Jesus rebuked the disciples. Then, *"[Jesus] took the children in his arms, put his hands on them and blessed them"* (Mark 10:16). When you take the time to train your children, you keep them from making the mistakes you made.

Obed-Edom Reversed the Curse

Obed-Edom reversed the generational curse over his family. Marilyn Hickey, in her book *Breaking Generational Curses* explained how generational curses can be broken. A generational curse is any sinful tendency that is passed down from one generation to the next, affecting the members of the family in succeeding generations. In each family tree, there are many traits which are passed down from generation to generation. Examples of generational curses include: hereditary illnesses, attitudes, and negative behavioral characteristics.

Doctors acknowledge the reality of generational curses when they ask, "Is there any history of heart problems in your family?" "Diabetes?" "Cancer?" "Arthritis?" "Chronic Pain?" Doctors understand that if there are health problems in your family background, you are likely to have the same problems.

Many families repeatedly suffer with problems of alcoholism, divorce, adultery, debt, obesity, teenage pregnancy, nervous breakdowns, anger, bitterness, or suicide. If a mother struggles with a particular sin, it is likely that her daughter will fight against the same temptations. If you research her history, you often find that the grandmother and even her great-grandmother dealt with the same problems.

Here is how it happens. One person repeatedly gives in to a particular temptation until the sin becomes a lifestyle. The sin becomes entrenched as a weakness toward a particular behavior. As Satan is allowed a foothold in the household, he controls the next generation by exploiting the same weakness. Eventually, the control Satan has over the mind, the will, and the emotions in the family extends to future generations and becomes a generational curse.

A Tale of Two Families

There is a story about two families that illustrates the power of generational curses and blessings. Max Jukes was an atheist who married a godless woman in the 1700's. Of his 560 descendants who have been traced, 310 died as paupers, 150 became criminals, 7 were murderers, 100 were alcoholics, and more than half of the women were prostitutes. This man's descendants cost the United States government millions of dollars in welfare and prison expenses.

Jonathan Edwards was a famous preacher and a committed Christian who was a contemporary of Max Jukes. He married a godly woman. Of his 1,394 descendants who have been traced, 295 graduated from college and 56 became professors. Thirty became judges, 100 were lawyers, 75 became military officers, 100 were famous as missionaries, preachers, or authors. Three were elected as U.S. senators, 3 as state governors, and some were sent as ministers to foreign countries, another 80 were elected to public office, 3 became mayors of large cities, 1 was the comptroller of the United States Treasury, and 1 even became the vice president of the United States. Jonathan Edwards passed a godly heritage down to his children, Max Jukes did not.

A wicked life can negatively affect your descendants for up to four generations. The Bible says, *"...the iniquity of the fathers* [can be visited] *upon the children to the third and fourth generations of those who hate* [God]*"* (Exodus 20:5 NKJV).

A righteous person creates a heritage of blessing for a thousand generations of descendants. *"...he is the faithful God, keeping his covenant of love to a thousand generations of those who love him and keep his commands"* (Deuteronomy 7:9). When we serve God wholeheartedly, we create a tradition of blessing to pass down to future generations. Because of your faithfulness to God, He will bless your family for a thousand generations to come.

God is a generational God.

God is a generational God. He blesses from generation to generation. Paul tells Timothy to pass on what he has learned to those who can pass it on to others. *"...the things you have heard me* (Paul is first generation) *say in the presence of many witnesses* (Timothy is part of the second generation) *entrust to reliable men* (third generation) *who will also be qualified to teach others* (fourth generation)" (2 Timothy 2:2).

The Curse of Edom

In order to see how generational curses work, let us trace the history of the curse on the Edomite side of Obed-Edom's family. Why were the Edomites cursed? Their story begins in the Book of Genesis. After the flood, Noah planted vineyards and distilled fermented wine. He got drunk. His son Ham saw him lying naked and told his brothers about it. When Noah awoke, he pronounced a curse on Canaan, the son of Ham. Canaan's descendants became the Canaanites. Isaac, the son of Abraham, had two sons, Esau and Jacob. God changed Jacob's name to Israel and he became the father of the Israelites. His brother Esau married two Canaanite women (against the wishes of his family) and became the father of the Edomites. The curse on the Edomites extended all the way back to the sin of Ham.

Generational curses tend to become more grievous as they touch new generations. Until the curse is broken, each generation sinks deeper into sin than the previous one. For example, statistics tell us that when parents divorce, their children are even more likely to divorce.

Throughout the Old Testament, every time we read about the Edomites, they are bad news. They were continually fighting with the Israelites (2 Chronicles 21:9; 25:14; 28:17), and they laughed when Jerusalem was conquered by the Babylonians (Psalm 137:7). Because of their wickedness God promised, *"For three sins of Edom, even for four, I will not turn back my wrath, because he pursued his brother with a sword, stifling all compassion, because his anger raged continually and his fury flamed unchecked"* (Amos 1:11).

Obed-Edom's Natural Heritage

The last Edomite we know about in history was Herod the Great. He was half Edomite and half Israelite. Throughout his life, there was a battle between his good side and bad side. God kept trying to break the curse in this family. The wise men came to King Herod and told him the prophecy about a messiah being born in Bethlehem. What did Herod do? He killed all the babies in Bethlehem.

Herod the Great had a son, Herod Antipas. John the Baptist witnessed to him (Mark 6:20). What did he do? He cut off John's head and continued his father's heritage of violence.

A third Herod, known as Herod Agrippa, threw Peter in prison. An angel released Peter, but Herod, instead of repenting, killed the guards who were responsible for guarding him. Again we see the curse rear its ugly head.

Finally, Herod Agrippa II, the fourth generation of the Herod family, had many conversations with Paul. In the saddest words of the Bible, he told Paul, *"You almost persuade me to become a Christian"* (Acts 26:28 NKJV). God kept trying to redeem this family, but they kept giving in to the curse of their heritage. Herod Agrippa II was the last in the lineage. History tells us he lost his position as ruler in Israel and bought a farm on the side of Mount Vesuvius to finish his life in disgrace. This proved to be a bad choice because when Mount Vesuvius erupted, it destroyed the countryside and that was the end of the Herod family. Today, there are no living members of the Herod family or anyone who claims to be an Edomite.

In every generation, God gives an opportunity for the curse to be broken. But, when people rebel against God, their sinful tendencies are passed down to their children. In each succeeding generation, the curse intensifies. Only submission to God can break the effects of the curse.

You Can Reverse the Curse

Obed-Edom reversed the curse on his family. His history as an Edomite did not negatively affect the lives of his children. By allowing God to live in his house and by serving the house of God, he destroyed the curse and released blessing on his family.

Just like Obed-Edom, my father turned the destiny of my family around. When he was born, his last name was Krahl (pronounced "crawl"). As a child his schoolmates teased him, "Hey Krahl, why don't you crawl on the ground?" For many years my father suffered the indignity of his last name. One day as he was praying, God spoke to him. "In My eyes, you do not crawl. I made you to be a king." Because of this word my father decided to legally change the last name of our family. When I was ten years old, our family stood before a federal judge and officially changed our name. Ever since I have been called "King" which is a prophetic utterance over my life. I am royalty. I am a son of the King of kings. My father changed our family destiny by changing our family name.

How Can a Generational Curse Be Broken?

1. **Repent** of family sins. You can defeat hereditary weaknesses in your family by giving your life to Jesus. When you decide to follow Jesus you become a member of a new family, the family of God. *"Therefore, if anyone is in Christ, he is a new creation; the old has gone, the new has come!"* (2 Corinthians 5:17). Ultimately, all family curses and hereditary sins can be traced back to the sin of Adam and Eve in the Garden of Eden. But Jesus died on the cross to set us free from sin and from all the effects of sin. *"Christ redeemed us from the curse..."* (Galatians 3:13). When you become a believer in Jesus you get a blood transfusion. The blood of Jesus cleanses your bloodline and you start a new family tree that begins with God. *"So if the Son sets you free, you will be free indeed"* (John 8:36).

Jesus died on the cross to set us free from sin and from all the effects of sin.

2. **Forgive** those in your life who have hurt or abused you. When you forgive, it releases you from your ties to their problems. *"For if you forgive men when they sin against you, your heavenly Father will also forgive you"* (Matthew 6:14).

3. **Submit** to God's will for your life and renounce the devil's hold on your life. *"Submit yourselves, then, to God. Resist the devil, and he will flee from you"* (James 4:7). If your family has struggled with certain sinful tendencies, renounce your involvement in those activities. Turn away from sin and live a life of righteousness.

4. **Proclaim** words of blessing over your family.

God Will Bless Your Family

Do you want to build a family legacy? Does God's presence dwell in your house? When you pray, do your kids sense His presence? Do you consult with God when making family decisions? Do your kids see you apologize to God when you make mistakes? Do you talk to Him about big things and little things? Is God the ruling Member of your family?

The greatest blessing is when your whole family serves God. When everything else is gone, family is what is important. Only family is eternal. Your service in the house of God goes beyond your life, it affects your children and grandchildren.

Even if your parents never knew the blessing of God, you can reverse the direction your family is traditionally heading. You can give your children a history to be proud of. By serving in God's house you are setting an example for generations to come.

Obed-Edom's entire family is serving in the house of God, but guess what? His story is not finished yet.

CHAPTER 11

TRUSTED WITH TREASURE

"...All the gold and silver and all the articles
found in the temple of God...
had been in the care of Obed-Edom...."

(2 CHRONICLES 25:24)

King David peered through weary eyes at the loyal subjects and leaders assembled together in his throne room. He recognized friends who guarded him when King Saul was on the hunt to murder him. He noticed men who came to him troubled and in debt, but had been transformed into mighty warriors. He gazed at younger men who served faithfully as his scribes and foot soldiers. From across the kingdom these leaders gathered to listen to their king one last time.

A trumpet reverberated through the room. All present watched in hushed silence as their wizened ruler shuffled slowly to the podium. Though he looked ancient, the voice of the king was still strong and unwavering.

"Friends and countrymen, my greatest dream is to build a permanent house for the Lord. Ever since I brought the ark to Jerusalem, the house of God has been little more than a large tent. Now it is time to build a real temple. The Lord has told me that since I am a man of war, I cannot build His house. However, today I want to provide enough treasure so my son Solomon can build God a house worthy of His dwelling presence."

The leaders of Israel listened intently as David continued, "The temple of God will be magnificent! Gold will cover the walls; bronze pillars will stand out front. The priests will wear the finest linens. Men and women will come from across Israel to worship God."

"How will we pay for this gigantic project?" asked a financial advisor.

David responded, "I ask each of you to give generously. To set an example, I will give first. From my own personal treasure house, I give all that I have for the building of the temple."

The crowd gasped as servants began piling treasure at the front of the room. One ton of gold, two tons of silver, six tons of bronze, and more precious stones than could be counted.

The news spread throughout Israel of the king's example of generosity for the house of God. The leaders and citizens of all backgrounds brought wealth from their own storehouses until their total contributions exceeded the king's giving. The treasure piled up until it was more than anyone had ever seen before.

When the people finished giving, David rejoiced greatly. Tears of joy streamed down his wrinkled cheeks as he imagined the splendor of the temple Solomon would build. An enormous amount of money had been raised.

"Who should I put in charge of the temple treasury?" King David asked himself. "I need a faithful servant who will know how to handle money. It must be an accountable steward who has the spirit of a giver and who has proven leadership skills."

As King David reviewed his choices, he remembered the wise man, Obed-Edom. So many years prior, Obed-Edom's life had been changed when God's presence came to live in his house.

Ever since Obed-Edom had served faithfully in the house of God in Jerusalem.

David called for Obed-Edom. He had been one of the first leaders to give in the offering. "My faithful and loyal servant whom God has blessed, I put you in charge of the temple treasury."

"Thank you, King David, my family and I will be faithful stewards of what the people have given so generously."

Obed-Edom remembered the day King David brought the ark to Jerusalem. He remembered how David had danced before the Lord with abandon because the king had the same love for God that he had discovered. He whispered to the king, "We are both addicted to God's presence. I will do my best to wisely use this treasure to build a magnificent house for the One we love."

In the final years of his long life Obed-Edom was entrusted with unprecedented wealth. This was a reward for his faithfulness in serving the house of God. Because of his generous giving, God gave to him.

Blessed Beyond Your Wildest Dreams!

Do you want God to entrust you with unprecedented blessing? He will if you put the principles found in this book into practice in your life.

The final time Obed-Edom's name appears in the Bible, we find he is the keeper of the temple treasury. This is not a small promotion, but a very big one. When King David took up the offering to build the temple the great men of Israel gave gold, silver, bronze, and precious stones worth over $2.5 billion in today's market prices. The Bible says, "David rejoiced greatly," which is the understatement of the millennium. Imagine how your pastor would celebrate if he took up a 2.5 billion dollar offering!

King David took this massive treasure and placed it in the hands of the man named Obed-Edom. He became the most trusted person in all of David's realm. This speaks of character, great trust, and an impeccable image.

Churches do not put the church treasury in the hands of any random person. Church leadership looks for someone who has served God faithfully for many years, who has been a consistent giver in the church, who has a servant's heart and desires to be a blessing to the congregation. They try to find someone who has enough money of their own to know how to properly handle the church's money. Because Obed-Edom was trusted with this position, we know he was a faithful servant, a

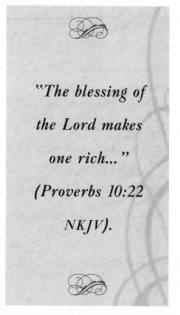

"The blessing of the Lord makes one rich..." (Proverbs 10:22 NKJV).

big giver (a big portion of the 2.5 billion dollars probably came from his own storehouse), and he was wealthy in his own right. Pretty impressive for someone who was once known as a slave. He was once the enemy of Israel, now he is entrusted with the wealth of Israel.

Obed-Edom went:

- From shame to fame.
- From nobody to somebody.
- From zero to a hero.
- From victim to victor.
- From chump to champ.
- From a slave to the king's treasurer.

God can do the same for you!

This is the last stage of spiritual promotion, when God releases unprecedented blessing into your hands. When you are faithful with what God gives you now, the day will come when God will pour out more blessing than you can receive. *"The blessing of the Lord makes one rich"* (Proverbs 10:22 NKJV).

The job of a steward is to care for what belongs to another.

Stewardship

When he was placed in charge of the temple treasury, Obed-Edom was entrusted with great wealth. The wealth was his to guard and to use for God's house. He was not an owner of the wealth, he was merely a steward of it. Obed-Edom would have been mistaken to use the temple wealth to build himself a new house.

The job of a steward is to care for what belongs to another. Stewards are always held accountable for the assets placed in their care. Stewardship is both a privilege and a responsibility. Good stewards will be given more; bad stewards will have what they were entrusted with taken away.

God has also given you stewardship of everything you possess. You are a steward. God has entrusted you with time, creativity, ability, talents, and wealth, which He expects you to use for His glory. You may think you own your possessions, but they are only on loan from God. We have a short period of time here on this earth to prove our trustworthiness. As stewards, we must be faithful. *"...it is required in stewards that one be found faithful"* (1 Corinthians 4:2 NKJV).

When we realize that we have stewardship, not ownership, it changes the way we use our wealth. Some make the mistake of thinking that God's blessings are simply for the enhancement of their own lives. They buy expensive watches, beautiful houses, new cars, and eat lavishly. While it is fine to own things, it is wrong to let things own you.

There has been a great misunderstanding among some Christians concerning the purpose of wealth. Wealth is not given so we can live a luxurious lifestyle. Rather, wealth is given so we can use it to help others.

What is God's definition of wealth? *"...God is able to make all grace abound to you, so that in all things at all times, having all that you need, you will abound in every good work"* (2 Corinthians 9:8). God puts wealth in our hands so we can use it as a tool to bless others. God wants to do this same miracle for you. He wants you to have plenty to cover all your needs with enough money left over that you can give to every good work.

What is the purpose of wealth? Abraham was blessed so he could be a blessing to others (Genesis 12:2-3). If you are willing to give to others, God will give to you. If God knows He can get it THROUGH you, then He will get it TO you.

This is why I am extremely careful as a minister with every dollar given to our ministry. Every dollar is a sacred trust from people who have worked hard to earn it and given it to be used to tell people about Jesus. I know if I am a faithful steward with little, God will be able to trust me with much.

As you prove yourself faithful with the small things, God will promote you to a place where you will be responsible for big things. Once you prove you can handle one dollar, God can potentially release hundreds, thousands, or even millions of dollars into your hands. You could become the recipient of unprecedented wealth.

What Would You Do with $1,000,000?

I recently daydreamed about what I would do if I had a million dollars to give to charity. I planned to give $100,000 to my church and $100,000 to my favorite missionary and $100,000 to a needy family. God broke into my daydreaming session and asked me, "What are you going to do with the twenty-dollar bill in your pocket?"

I replied to God, "I am going to use it for my lunch today."

God asked, "Why don't you give it away?"

"Because I need it to pay for lunch," I explained to Him.

The Lord replied, "Daniel, if you give the twenty, someday I will trust you to give a million, but if you cannot skip a lunch in obedience to Me, you will never have a million to give."

I gave the money away and fasted lunch that day. I learned that obedience in the small things brings opportunity for big things. The important question for you to ask yourself is not, "What would I do if I had a million dollars?" but "What am I doing with the twenty dollars I have in my pocket?"

According to Winston Churchill, "We make a living by what we earn but we make a life by what we give." Robert Louis Stevenson said, "Do not judge today by the harvest you reap but by the seeds you sow." Zig Ziglar points out, "You'll always have everything you want in life if you'll help enough other people get what they want."

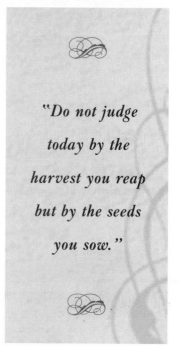

"Do not judge today by the harvest you reap but by the seeds you sow."

If You Give to God, How Will He Bless You?

As you are faithful giving to God, He will be faithful to bless you. Deuteronomy 28 has a list of many ways God will reward you for your faithfulness. I rewrote the passage for modern times.

All these blessings will come upon you and follow you wherever you go if you obey the LORD your God: You will be blessed in the city and blessed in the suburbs. Your children will be blessed (they will do well in school, in sports, and in church). They will be obedient and will grow in wisdom, stature, and in favor with God and man.

The wages of your job will increase, you will receive raises from your boss and year-end bonus checks. The interest rate on your savings account will double, your credit card bills will be paid off. Your real estate will increase in value. Your mortgage will be reduced. You will get better jobs. Your promotions will come quickly. Your work will be fulfilling and your compensation levels will be out of sight. God will bless your diligence and you will have to work less and less for more and more results.

You will have God concepts, insights, and creative ideas for wealth creation and increase. Your strategies will produce abundance for those around you. You will have favor with authorities. You will have prosperous relationships.

Your books will be best-sellers. Your songs will earn royalties. Your movies will receive rave reviews and become blockbusters. Your inventions will be purchased by thousands of people.

Your creative ideas will generate wealth. You will make record-breaking sales and your commissions will rise. You will receive estates and inheritances. You will be awarded scholarships and grants.

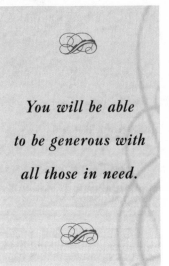

You will be able to be generous with all those in need.

You will have more than enough to give into the Kingdom of God and promote the gospel of Jesus Christ. You will be able to be generous with all those in need. You will support missionaries and give significantly to your church building fund. Your dollars will result in souls being won.

Your spouse will love you all the days of your life and divorce will not darken your marriage nor threaten your financial status. Your shopping baskets shall overflow. You will find great deals when you are shopping for food. You will find bargain discounts on name-brand clothing. Your cooking will taste great and your food will multiply so you can feed extra people. You will be blessed when you arrive at work and when you leave for the day.

The LORD will grant that the enemies who rise up against you will be defeated before you. They will come at you from one direction but flee from you in seven. Those who are suing you will drop their cases. Your creditors will forgive your debts. The IRS will rule in your favor. You shall receive warnings but not tickets from policemen.

The LORD will send a blessing on your savings accounts, your checking accounts, your IRAs, and your 401k's. Your investments, your stocks, your bonds, and your mutual funds will multiply in value. Everything you put your hand to (including your hobbies, your jobs, your entrepreneurial ideas) will be blessed.

The LORD your God will bless you in the land He is giving you. You will find great deals when purchasing your family home, real estate, rental properties, and commercial properties. The LORD will establish you as His holy people, as He promised you on oath, if you keep the commands of the LORD your God and walk in His ways. The LORD will grant you abundant prosperity, in the talents of your children, the increase of your investments, and the granting of a lifetime source of income in the land He swore to your forefathers to give you.

You will be healthy all the days of your life. The LORD will make you the head, not the tail. If you pay attention to the commands of the LORD your God that I give you this day and carefully follow them, you will always be at the top, never at the bottom. You will be a landlord, not a renter; a lender, not a borrower; and a giver, not a taker. The LORD will open the heavens, the storehouse of His bounty, to send rain on your land in season and to bless all the work of your hands. Then all the peoples on earth will see that you are called by the name of the LORD (Christians), and they will be amazed at your prosperity.

Seek God's Presence, Not His Presents

We see Obed-Edom being blessed throughout this book. But Obed-Edom was never seeking material blessing, he was seeking God's presence.

Then the blessing came. If we focus on the blessing, we miss the Blesser. If you just read this book searching for material blessing (health, wealth, happiness), you will miss the greater blessing, the presence of God.

As you serve in the presence of God, you cannot help being blessed. As you are faithful, God is able to trust you and is able to release unprecedented blessing into your hands.

Now Obed-Edom has been trusted to care for the temple treasury and guess what? This is the last time he is mentioned in the Bible, but his story is not finished yet. The story of the blessing of Obed-Edom continues today in YOUR life!

Epilogue:
Your Story Is Not Finished Yet

Before you put this book down, take a moment to inventory all the blessings of God in your life. How has God's presence changed your life? I am sure God has done many wonderful miracles for you and blessed you countless times.

But guess what?

Your story is not finished yet! You are still in the first few pages of God's story for your life. The half has not been told. God writes the greatest stories, better than your favorite fairy tale and He wants to continue writing a great story through your life. The most famous author in the universe wants to write a happily-ever-after ending to your story.

The blessings of your past are nothing compared to the blessings God has planned for you. The Apostle Paul said, *"No eye has seen, no ear has heard, no mind has conceived what God has prepared for those who love him"* (1 Corinthians 2:9).

The story of Obed-Edom is similar to the life of every successful believer. He came from a bad background, but God's presence changed his life. Because of God's blessing upon his house, he began to serve in the house of God. As he proved his faithfulness, he is promoted again and again until he finished his journey with enormous resources under his control.

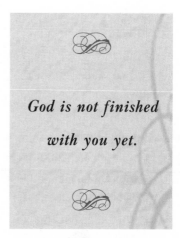

God is not finished with you yet.

What was his secret? Staying close to the presence of God through faithful service.

I do not know where you are on your journey. Perhaps you recently invited God to live in your house or perhaps you have been serving God faithfully for many years. Regardless of where you are on your path, God is not finished with you yet.

This book about Obed-Edom reveals how simple it is to be a successful Christian. It is not complicated, not lots of do's and don'ts, nor lots of mysterious keys for success. Just get into God's presence, then be faithful in finding a place to serve in your local church. As you allow God to live in your house and continue to serve faithfully in God's house, you will be blessed beyond your wildest dreams. If God promoted Obed-Edom from the position of a slave to keeper of the temple treasury, imagine what God wants to do for you!

Today the blessing of Obed-Edom is activated in your life. Today is your Promotion Day. Congratulations! Your story is just getting started!

"...he who began a good work in you will carry it on to completion until the day of Christ Jesus" (Philippians 1:6).

Resources to Help You Grow

You can be Healed

When you need healing, listen to this CD. Discover the truths that will help you tap into God's healing power!

(CD 01) $15.00

The Blessing of Obed-Edom

This is the #1 message that the Body of Christ needs to hear. You will learn the explosive secrets to your supernatural promotion!

(DVD 01) $20.00

7 Reasons to be a Soulwinner

Daniel King's passion is to lead the lost to Christ. Learn how to ignite the same passion in your life. Plus: Practical tips for witnessing.

(CD 02) $15.00

Thinking Outside the BOX

God is not in the BOX. Learn why on this powerful CD that will change the way you think about God.

(CD 03) $15.00

Ignite

A must for those who want to ignite genuine passion for Jesus! Discover the keys to sparking your personal revival.

(CD 04) $15.00

Crowns

Do you wonder what your reward will be in heaven? This CD will explain how you can receive your eternal prize!

(CD 05) $15.00

To Order Call: 1-877-431-4276 Write: PO Box 701113 Tulsa, OK 74170
Online: www.kingministries.com

6 Power-Packed Books

Healing Power

Do you need healing? This power-packed book contains 17 truths to activating your healing today!

(BK 02) $20.00

Fire Power

Inside these pages you will learn how to CATCH the fire of God, KEEP the fire of God, and SPREAD the fire of God!

(BK 01) $12.00

Soul Winning

Do you have a passion for the lost? This book shares over 150 truths about soul winning.

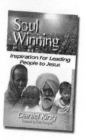

(BK 05) $10.00

The Secret of Obed-Edom

Unlock the secret to supernatural promotion and a more intimate walk with God. Unleash amazing blessing in your life!

(BK 06) $20.00

Power of the Seed

Discover the power of Seedtime & Harvest! Discover why your giving is the most important thing you will ever do!

(BK 04) $20.00

Welcome to the Kingdom

This is a perfect book for new believers. Learn how to be saved, healed, and delivered. (Available in bulk discounts)

(BK 03) $10.00

To Order Call: 1-877-431-4276 Write: PO Box 701113 Tulsa, OK 74170
Online: www.kingministries.com

The Secret of Obed-Edom is available in bulk
for your bookstore, church leadership,
volunteers, Sunday school classes, and members.

Call: 1-877-431-4276 for church discounts

ORDER FORM

Name: _____

Church: _____

Address: _____

State/Province: _____ Zip Code: _____

Phone: _____

E-mail: _____

Yes! Please send me the following products:

Product #	Title	Quantity	Total

S&H: _____

Total: _____

Please include $5.00 shipping and handling for each item ordered

❑ Yes! I want to join the MillionHeirs' Club and help Daniel & Jessica King win 1,000,000 souls to Jesus every year.

Enclosed is my gift of:

❑ $100   ❑ $50   ❑ $500   ❑ $1,000   ❑ Other: _____

❑ Yes! I want to make a monthly pledge of $ _____

Please charge my: ❑ VISA or ❑ MASTERCARD

_ _ _ _ - _ _ _ _ - _ _ _ _ - _ _ _ _

Expiration Date: _ _ / _ _ Signature: _____

To order Daniel King's books fill out this page and mail it to:
King Ministries International
P. O. Box 701113 • Tulsa, OK 74170-1113 • www.kingministries.com

ABOUT THE AUTHOR:

Daniel King and his wife Jessica met in the middle of Africa while they were both on a mission trip. They are in high demand as speakers at churches and conferences all over North America. Their passion, energy, and enthusiasm are enjoyed by audiences everywhere they go.

They are international missionary evangelists who do massive soul-winning festivals in countries around the world. Their passion for the lost has taken them to over fifty nations preaching the gospel to crowds that often exceed 50,000 people.

Daniel's story is much like the story of Obed-Edom. His faithfulness to serve God has given him greater and greater opportunities for service. He was called into the ministry when he was five years old and began to preach when he was six. His parents became missionaries to Mexico when he was ten. When he was fourteen he started a children's ministry that gave him the opportunity to minister in some of America's largest churches while still a teenager.

At the age of fifteen, Daniel read a book where the author encouraged young people to set a goal to earn $1,000,000. Daniel reinterpreted the message and determined to win 1,000,000 people to Christ every year.

Daniel has authored nine books including his best sellers *Healing Power* and *Fire Power*. His book *Welcome to the Kingdom* has been given away to tens of thousands of new believers.